TEACHING
to
Wonder

RESPONDING
TO POETRY
IN THE
SECONDARY
CLASSROOM

·················

CARL LEGGO

PACIFIC EDUCATIONAL PRESS

Published by Pacific Educational Press
Faculty of Education, University of British Columbia
Vancouver, Canada V6T 1Z4
Telephone (604) 822-5385
Facsimile (604) 822-6603

The publisher would like to acknowledge the financial contribution made by Canadian Heritage towards the support of its publishing program.

Canadian Cataloguing in Publication Data
Leggo, Carleton Derek, 1953-
  Teaching to wonder

  Includes bibliographical references and index.
  ISBN 1-895766-31-1

  1. Poetry--Study and teaching (Secondary) II. Title.
PN1101.L43 1997   808.1'071'2   C97-910440-8

Editing by Carolyn Sale
Cover design by Warren Clark
Printed and bound in Canada

97 98 99 10 9 8 7 6 5 4 3 2 1

For Lana
who knows poetry in her heart
who knows the heart of poetry

Author's Acknowledgements

I thank Professors George Haley, Barry Cameron, Robert Gibbs, and Robert Hawkes at the University of New Brunswick, and Professors Jim Parsons, John Oster, and Margaret Iveson at the University of Alberta, for their instruction and encouragement. Also, I thank the editors of *English Journal, Reflections on Canadian Literacy, Alberta English,* and *Research Forum* who have generously supported my writing about poetry and teaching, and I thank the many students in school and university classrooms who have responded to my teaching poetry. Finally, I thank my editor Carolyn Sale, who shaped this book with wise insight and careful devotion.—Carl Leggo

CONTENTS

Poetry in the Classroom

As a student in school I believed that poetry was written by dead men who had lived in faraway countries. I also believed that poetry was about grand themes of love and war and heroism and religion and nature. Moreover, I thought that poetry was a puzzle—obscure, ambiguous, and convoluted—that I could never solve. I never wrote poetry in school because poetry was written by people with gifts for rhyme and rhythm, and I was convinced I had none.

As a secondary school English teacher for nine years I perpetuated many of the unproductive experiences with poetry I had known as a student. Now as a professor with responsibility for teaching English teachers, I hear from my students many stories about fear of poetry, dislike of poetry, and unpleasant experiences with reading poetry. Often I hear comments like "I don't understand poetry" and "I never read poetry."

Too often students' experiences in poetry classes are similar to my experiences in driving school. For four Saturdays I sat in a classroom and listened to lectures and watched films that depicted the driving process in intricate detail. My first experience behind the wheel of a real car was a shock. I understood the mechanics of driving and had driven hundreds of miles in my imagination, but suddenly realized that I could not drive. Too many poetry classes operate around the model of my driving school experience. The teacher creates an artificial environment in which readers are granted entry to the poetic text through the door of his or her perspective. Armed with a battery of notes and a special guidebook, the teacher gives a lesson designed to manipulate the students to reiterate the teacher's encounter with the poem in the hope that meticulous and appropriate attention to two dozen poems a year will prepare the reader for reading poetry with satisfaction and enthusiasm. It is not surprising that most students learn only an antipathy for reading poetry.

In the last three decades there has been a ferment (perhaps a "revolution" is more apt) in literary theory. Fundamental assumptions about language, literature, knowledge, reality, and personality have been re-examined, exploded, and reconstructed. The study of literature has been interwoven with studies in linguistics, anthropology, sociology, history, psychoanalysis, philosophy, and politics. Never in the history of literary studies has so much attention been devoted to issues of theory. Yet this current eruption of interest in theory has had only a minimal influence on the practice of English teaching in secondary schools. Many university professors are not interested in the pedagogical possibilities of the new theories. They are engaged in running a closed circuit of debate— an invigorating activity but not especially useful. And many secondary teachers of English are intimidated by theory; it seems abstract, incomprehensible, distant from the world of the classroom.

Perhaps the most important aspect of theory that needs to be acknowledged is that no teaching occurs without a theoretical foundation. Whether teachers recognize it or not, theory undergirds all their efforts even if the theory is unarticulated or only partially understood. Catherine Belsey's observation is a timely reminder that theory is operative in the practice of reading as well:

> What we do when we read, however "natural" it seems, presupposes a whole theoretical discourse, even if unspoken, about language and about meaning, about the relationships between meaning and the world, meaning and people, and finally about people themselves and their place in the world. (Belsey, 1980, 4)

Since this is the case, teachers and students need a clearly formulated, intelligently understood theoretical infrastructure for success in their teaching and reading. They need to be more reflexive about their teaching and reading practices and the assumptions that guide their practices. Josie Levine observes that:

> change does not happen by virtue of one insightful theoretical leap nor by the spread of theoretical ideas alone. Individual teachers have to learn and think about theory, take steps to

8

implement it, reflect upon their practice and develop it. Moreover, each new generation of teachers has this learning to do and needs a climate which encourages it. (Levine, 1984, 46)

For meeting this need the current academic interest in literary theory has generated a treasure trove of terminology, concepts, and perspectives that can refurbish English instruction and experience in secondary schools. Why should university English departments have all the good theories? It is time that a firmer connection be established between university and school classrooms.

Current literary theories are not a panacea for all the demanding needs related to English instruction in schools, however. Nor is there a single theory that can be readily modified or structured for teaching poetry. In a sense my approach to modern literary theory is similar to the way we shop. I select from among the diverse items available in the Emporium of Literary Theory and offer a few of them to you in this book. In making my selections I will be intent on justifying my choices, but it is not possible to engage in a full-fledged, vigorous debate with all the different branches of modern literary theory. Hundreds of books and essays have already been written, and each year the list multiplies. At any rate, I am not enamoured with any one single theory. My attraction is, instead, to the possibilities the new theories provide, possibilities for reading, writing, understanding, evaluating, and teaching poetry with enhanced awareness and appreciation of the texts as texts, as well as engagement with the social, political, and cultural contexts in which texts are written and read, and published, reviewed, and taught. I want to use the resources of modern literary theory to lead me, and others, out of the thicket of unsatisfying poetry experiences.

There is an element of presumption in my claim that I can propose strategies for more effective and satisfying poetry instruction. The claim rings with a bold confidence, the kind of confidence a person might know while watching a heavyweight boxing match on television dreaming about what he or she would do if boxing in the ring. Armchair confidence is only easy braggadocio, false and futile, appropriately ignored. Whether presumptuous or pragmatic, I still contend that my proposals have a rich potential for the teaching of poetry. A consideration of some of the ways that a teacher might proceed with the ideas will help disperse fears about presumption and pragmatism, new burdens and old ideas.

But, first, we need to reflect on the dynamics of the typical classroom. Recommendations that call for radical reforms of schooling will fall on deaf ears unless those reforms can attract or be initiated by teachers and implemented by teachers in actual classrooms. For that reason the expression "student-centred approach" can be misleading and threatening because it implies a diminishing of the role of the teacher. A more promising approach to classroom life recognizes the central role of the teacher while proposing that the student, the text, and the world also ought to be considered centres of circles that intersect with the circle in which the teacher stands The classroom entails interrelationships that must all be held in balance. If the student is thrust forward as the centre of the classroom, there is rightly concern that the student will dictate the complexion of schooling instead of schooling contributing to the student's complexion. Or if too much attention is directed towards texts, then students' particular needs might be ignored because of a dedication to completing the presentation of the texts. The world obviously influences the classroom, but the classroom ought also to influence the world. The world of students cannot be locked outside the classroom door. But at the same time the students' world is too narrow and needs to be expanded by schooling.

Charged with creating an environment where this balance can be actualized is the classroom teacher. Continuing education, reflection on experiences, a persistent commitment to experimentation, and a willingness to change are all qualities of a professional attitude, and teachers need to manifest these attitudes.

Robin Barrow in *Giving Teaching Back to Teachers* argues convincingly for "a situation in which teachers are both expected to, and competent to, make most of their decisions about what to teach and how to teach themselves." (Barrow, 1984, 261) Curriculum guides, curriculum consultants, principals, professors and scholars can map out the terrain and recommend directions to pursue, but in classrooms teachers daily make decisions about what and how they are going to teach. A classroom is not like a locomotive that can be driven along prescribed rails. It is more like a marriage. It is about relationships and maturing in relationships, about commitment and struggle, about caring and communicating. How successfully a marriage progresses depends on the people involved. In the case of a classroom the teacher has the primary responsibility for creating an environment conducive to a productive working relationship. Obviously many classrooms fail to function in this way, but evidence of failure does not refute the contention that the essential business of the classroom is to provide an environment for reflection, and a venue for discussions about experience and life.

The book proposes several strategies by which poetry might be used to these ends. I have used these strategies with my students in secondary school as well as with my students in university classes, and I have shared them at teacher conferences as well as with parents. In addition to practical strategies for the teaching of poetry in the secondary classroom, I provide an overview of four theoretical perspectives that support and inform them. The practical strategies are thus grounded in a comprehensible discussion of theory. Practice and theory need to ride in tandem, each supporting and complementing the other.

It is possible to read the book for practical strategies to use with a grade ten class on Monday morning. And it is also possible to read the book for an overview of several current theoretical perspectives. But the most effective way to read it is probably with a clear sense of the book's overarching design.

The book explores four main theoretical perspectives. The perspective most familiar to English language arts teachers is the reader-response approach. This approach to reading literature has been popular in many classrooms for at least a decade, but it is an approach that has been ignored or rejected by many teachers who think that it fails to pay sufficient attention to the complexity of a poem. In brief, many teachers think that the reader-response approach to reading poetry only invites subjective and personal responses that ignore the textual qualities of a poem as well as the social, cultural, and political contexts in which poems are written and published and read. With these concerns in mind, I expand on the reader-response approach with several less familiar theoretical perspectives, among them semiotics, deconstruction, and cultural criticism. Semiotics focusses on a poem as a network of signs or textual devices. Deconstruction reveals how texts can be interpreted in multiple ways. Finally, cultural criticism helps readers explore the ways that a poetic text is written and read and taught and understood in social, cultural, historical, and political contexts that are constantly changing. In short, my aim is to promote a reader-response approach to reading poetry which pays careful attention to the complex dynamics of the interactions among readers and poets and poetic texts and cultural contexts.

The book begins with the basic question, What is a poem?, and seeks to expand some of the parameters that typically constrain conceptions of poetry. Next, I elucidate the reader-response approach by comparing it to the New Critical approach, which was the dominant way of teaching and reading poetry in school and university classrooms for many years. I then develop several strategies for inviting students to respond personally to poetry. These strategies are intended to be non-threatening and fun. They do not require a great deal of class time and commitment. They are warm-up activities that will help students dispel some misconceptions about poetry.

Following the strategies that introduce reader-response approaches, I focus on the theoretical perspective of semiotics in order to present ways of instructing students to respond to poetry with greater awareness of the poem as a network of signs that comprise a text.

Next, I present a thumbnail sketch of deconstruction as a way of reading poetry, and I describe and illustrate several approaches that demonstrate the kind of reading that is called deconstructive. This is likely the toughest part of the book, but my commitment is to finding a balance between theory and practice, and I do not want to shy away from deconstruction because it is complicated. Reading poetry is a complicated enterprise. I suggest ways of responding to poems that refuse to take anything for granted, ways that defer closure in order to keep the poem open for ongoing and plural responses.

Finally, in discussing the theoretical perspective of cultural criticism, I propose that all reading and writing is influenced by ideological dynamics. I hope that by the time teachers and students come to this last section, they will be enthusiastic performers of poems, personally convinced that poetry is inextricably connected to their lives and experiences and confident about their skills for responding to poetry.

This book is not intended to be just a how-to book, a manual for teaching and reading poetry. The strategies are not intended to comprise a full-fledged poetry unit. They are guides for the teacher. But decisions about how much time will be devoted to each strategy, whether or not to use all the strategies, and what poetry will be read are primarily the teacher's responsibility. Though it isn't essential to follow the strategies in the sequence I have developed, each successive strategy expands on the previous strategies. Nor are the strategies autonomous lesson plans which can be completed and dismissed. They are interconnected like the parts of the body each performing its function in the whole.

The poems I include have been selected from a wide variety of sources. I am opposed to the use of one poetry anthology for an entire class. Instead teachers and students need access to numerous sources of poetry including anthologies and literary journals. At the end of the book I include a list of anthologies I regard as particularly useful. Libraries and bookstores can be combed for poetry, and teachers and students can stuff file folders full of favourite poems. Then the poems used in class will be poems selected by the teacher and the students.

The main reason I am opposed to the use of a single anthology (or only a few anthologies) is that every anthology is coloured by its editor's preferences and prejudices. In his introduction to the *Oxford Book of Contemporary Verse* the well-known poet D.J. Enright explains: "The present anthology contains no 'confessional' poetry . . . since if poetry is a public matter it is not the place for private revelations, and if it is not a public matter it has no place in a published book." (Enright, 1980, xxx) I am bewildered and frustrated by Enright's bias against "confessional" poetry. A published poem, regardless of its subject, becomes a public affair. What Enright effectively does in his anthology is omit poetry that has an overtly emotional or personal voice, the kind of poetry that women like Anne Sexton, Stevie Smith, and Adrienne Rich write, the kind of poetry to which many adolescents will readily respond. The way to avoid biases and open up diverse vistas on poetry is to use as many poems from as many sources as time and resources permit.

Having complained about Enright's bias, I must also confess my own bias concerning the poems I use in the explanation of the strategies. I have concentrated on contemporary poems in part because I think twentieth-century poetry is a useful way to attract young readers to the diversity and unpredictability of the poetic genre. But perhaps the most significant reason is that much contemporary poetry is ignored. Increasingly it seems that the only people reading poetry are poets. Students need to be exposed to the writing of young poets, need to be reminded that poetry is no antiquated use of language suitable only to an age without television or VCRs. Only then will they be able to appreciate the power of older poetic language. I can still remember, for example, the experience of reading, for the first time, one of John Donne's "Holy Sonnets." My tears taught me a lesson not to be forgotten. Extending across the centuries and an ocean, trespassing the boundaries of one world and stretching into another, Donne's words continue to exercise their power in the lives of readers, generation after generation. It is that experience, ultimately, that I hope to share.

CHAPTER 1

What Is a Poem?

Of the many barriers blocking response to poetry, perhaps none is more formidable than the set of expectations that students bring to the experience of reading poetry. Ellen Strenski and Nancy Giller Esposito explored the expectations of their students in an innovative research project with some startling conclusions. They asked their students to read two unsigned poems, one "generated at random by a computer, in turn based on a program of components blindly selected from anthologies" (Strenski and Esposito, 1980, 142) and one by Philip Levine. The students were asked to read the poems, even discuss them with friends, and then answer two questions: (1) decide which poem was generated by the computer and which was written by the poet and give reasons for their choices; and (2) choose the poem they preferred and explain their choice. In Strenski's class not only did fifteen out of thirty-two students identify the poems incorrectly (though most preferred Levine's poem), their explanations exposed an alarming number of misconceptions about poetry. Strenski summarized some of the recurring misconceptions:

> Only some subjects are suitable for poetry. . . . A conversational or intimate tone is inappropriate to poetry; only public melodrama is suitable. . . . Correct punctuation is good; poetry is good; therefore, poetry must be correctly punctuated. . . . Imagery is always non-literal. . . . Poetry must be ornate. . . . Poetry must have regular rhythm. (145-146)

Even more disturbing for Strenski was that "students . . . heard confusion in the computer poem, called it ambiguity, and met it with awe and respect. If they could not understand, the fault was theirs. Unintelligibility equalled profundity equalled better than they." (149)

Much of the difficulty students have with reading and responding to poetry is that they bring inadequate and inappropriate expectations and attitudes to their reading. After examining the responses of many students Patrick Dias concludes:

> What is immediately apparent as one glances through the protocols is that an individual's pattern of response does not vary from one poem to the next. It seems as though it is not so much the poem that dictates how it must be read; the reading is directed much more by the individual's expectations of how a poem means and the individual's beliefs about how one goes about making sense of a poem. Or, in other words, individual patterns of response appear to be determined primarily by the set of expectations and beliefs a reader brings to a poem. (Dias, 1985, 213)

Therefore, in order to expand and enlarge students' responses, their sets of expectations must be enlarged and expanded. To achieve that objective, students need exposure to a wide variety of poems. Found poems, prose poems, concrete poems, and sound poems broaden and develop students' expectations concerning poetry.

Found Poems

The following poem is a found poem.

The Courage to Love
by Carl Leggo

But
as the hand of love
               freely extended
always returns
covered with scars
 (if not nailed to a cross),
it is not stupid
to refuse the cure;
it is not stupid

to remain paralyzed,
stuck on the pallet.
But
it is boring.

I found this poem in an essay by the Reverend William Sloane Coffin. In the essay the words are written as a prose statement embedded in a paragraph with other prose statements. I have constructed a poem by rearranging the words. Readers might question the value or significance of this found poem, but they will likely agree that it looks like a poem.

As an item of interest and curiosity the found poem has been "found," anthologized, and discussed since the 1960s. It raises some vexing questions. Is a found poem really a poem? Is a found poem really plagiarism? Doesn't a found poem blow a big hole in the traditional myth of the original poet inspired by an unseen Muse? Couldn't anybody find poems? Is the world inundated with poems just waiting to be found?

Tom Hansen thinks that there is "little to say about the found or accidental poem" and that "most found poems are more dilute than even the flabbiest of made poems." (Hansen, 1980, 271) Hansen is at least partly correct: there isn't a whole lot to say about many found poems. Indeed that may be one of their distinct advantages. Why must every poem be discussed? But perhaps the primary advantage of found poems is that they encourage people to examine the effects of the shape and the structure of poems. The author of a found poem is transforming prose texts into poetry by playing with the space of the page, line lengths, and stanzaic structures.

A further benefit of found poems is that they can be fun. Consider the following found poem:

The Mystic East
by Robin Blaser

Jerry's Nose	Butter Cove
Come-by-Chance	Tea Cove
Blow-me-down	Sugar Loaf
Bumble Bee Bight	Cape Onion

Ha Ha Bay
Bleak Joke Cove
Nancy Oh
Joe Batt's Arm
Gripe Point
Bad Bay
Misery Point
Famish Gut
Confusion Bay
Empty Basket
Heart's Desire
Heart's Content
Safe Harbour
Sweet Bay
Little Paradise
Angel's Cove
Cupids
English Harbour
Portugal Cove
Harbour Breton
Frenchman's Cove
Ireland's Eye
Bay D'Espoir, heard as Bay Despair
Chaleur Bay
Plate Cove
Ladle Cove
Chimney Cove
Spoon Cove
Rooms
Bread Island
Cheese Island
Mistaken Point
God Bay
Sacred Bay
Devil Cove
Nick's Nose Cove

Turnip Cove
Mutton Bay
Black Island
Red Island
Green Island
White Bay
Orange Bay
Blue Cove
Grey Islands
Lion's Den
Bear Cove
Horse Chops
Hare's Ears Point
Dog Cove
Cat Gut
Seal's Nest Island
Dragon Bay
Fox Roost
Muskrat Brook
Goat Island
Goose Bay
Eagle Island
Trout River
Button Island
Shoe Cove
Stocking Harbour
Petticoat Island
Hatchet Cove
Sitdown Pond
Goblin
False Cape
God Almighty Cove
Nameless Cove
Harbour Harbour

(Historic Newfoundland

After examining Blaser's found poem with students, you might send your class on a scavenger hunt in search of poems. Washroom graffiti, memoranda from the principal's office, teachers' comments on report cards, health and physics textbooks, rule books for badminton, even juice cartons may yield poems. I found one of my favourite poems on a wall in the men's washroom in the Harriet Irving Library.

Everything you ever wanted to know about philosophy, but was too embarrassed to ask
by Carl Leggo

to Be is to Do
    Kant (the German school)
to Do is to Be
    Carlyle (the British school)
Do Be Do Be Do
    Sinatra (the American school)
Be a Do Bee
    Miss Ann (the Pre-school)

What is the value of found poems for teachers and students? Found poems are fun because they involve playing with words. Too many readers think that poetry must be serious and must deal with grand themes. Everybody can find poems in the texts that surround us all the time. Found poetry reminds us to open our eyes and see the possibilities for play and fun in the texts all around us. In this way, we expand our conventional expectations of what a poem is and can be.

Prose Poems

Unlike the found poem, which transforms prose into poetry, the prose poem transforms poetry into prose (or at least produces a hybrid that doesn't look much like poetry, but has a distinctly "poetic" tone). Perhaps the prose poem could be called "proetry". Michael Benedikt observes that "the prose poem is an international form that has been explored by major poets abroad for almost two centuries. Although a well-known, even venerable, genre world-wide, it is only recently that English-speaking poets, particularly Americans, have 'discovered' the prose poem." (Benedikt, 1976, 39)

The following prose poems raise interesting questions about what is a poem:

Moment in Autumn
by Michael Bullock

The trees are weeping tears of blood. The earth's sorrow rises in a billowing cloud of mist, in which the drowning sun strives despairingly to keep afloat. I see your face, fading like the sun, vanishing in the haze of distance. The cold and the melancholy of this afternoon of bare branches, black birds and reeds whispering in the grey water hold me in their grip and prevent me from stretching out my hand to draw you back. My voice is smothered by the heaving mist that extinguishes the final glimmer of the sun.

The Elm Log
by Alexander Solzhenitsyn

We were sawing firewood when we picked up an elm log and gave a cry of amazement. It was a full year since we had chopped down the trunk, dragged it along behind a tractor, and sawn it up into logs, which we had then thrown onto barges and wagons, rolled into stacks, and piled up on the ground–and yet this elm log had still not given up! A fresh green shoot had sprouted from it with a promise of a thick leafy branch, or even a whole new elm tree.

We placed the log on the sawing horse, as though on an executioner's block, but we could not bring ourselves to bite into it with our saw. How could we? That log cherished life as dearly as we did; indeed, its urge to live was even stronger than ours.

When you ask your students what these passages of prose have in common with poetry, you will probably receive a wide range of suggestions that focus on the expression of emotions in the poems. In "Moment in Autumn," Bullock uses the conventional device of pathetic fallacy so that nature is intimately identified with human emotions. The passage is stocked with a catalogue of vivid word-pictures that help create the effect of desolation: "weeping tears of blood," "drowning sun," "your face, fading like the sun," "sorrow," "billowing cloud of mist," "strives despairingly," "vanishing," "melancholy," "smothered," "heaving mist." Bullock spares no effort to describe the situation as desolate. Some readers might think he has overdone the description. Many adolescents not yet fortified against emotional crises will probably identify with Bullock's emotional reaction (and might even want to write a prose poem like his).

In what ways is Solzhenitsyn's "The Elm Log" different from and yet similar to Bullock's poem? Some students might suggest that the language is plainer, less embellished, more conversational. Many readers might conclude that "The Elm Log" is less "poetic" than "Moment in Autumn," but this is the kind of judgment that students need to be guided against making. There is no unique kind or quality of language that is distinctly the province of poetry.

So, why call "The Elm Log" a poem? It narrates an incident. It explores significant issues of hope, the refusal to surrender to death, the indomitable will to live, the respect engendered by the unflagging urge to live. But is "The Elm Log" a poem? Kent Thompson might call it a "postcard story," a very short, short story. Solzhenitsyn is well known for his lengthy and moving novels. "The Elm Log" could easily be an anecdotal passage from *The Cancer Ward* or *The First Circle*. Yet Michael Benedikt has included it in his anthology of prose poems.

Benedikt defines the prose poem as "a genre of poetry, self-consciously written in prose, and characterized by the intense use of virtually all the devices of poetry." (Benedikt, 1976, 47) Benedikt is careful to highlight "intense" because he recognizes that the devices of poetry (metaphor, symbol, rhythm) are typically also the devices of prose imagery.

What is a poem? is a slippery question. Perhaps the best response is, Well, I can't define it, but I know one when I see (hear) one. Perhaps a poem is what we agree is a poem, what we read as a poem. Perhaps our set of expectations determines whether or not we read/hear a collection of words as a poem. The best way to expand the set of expectations that students bring to their reading of poems is to provide them with frequent opportunities to read a wide range of poems.

Concrete Poems

Like found and prose poems, concrete poems extend the parameters of expectations about what a poem is. A concrete poem shapes and organizes language so that its design or layout on the page illustrates the subject of the poem. It is then a visual poem and sometimes even seems to militate against an oral reading. Mary Ellen Solt explains:

> There is a fundamental requirement which the various kinds of concrete poetry meet: concentration upon the physical material from which the poem or text is made. Emotions and ideas are not the physical materials of poetry. If the artist were not a poet he might be moved by the same emotions and ideas to make a painting (if he were a painter), a piece of sculpture (if he were a sculptor), a musical composition (if he were a composer). Generally speaking the material of the concrete poem is language. (Solt, 1970, 7)

Concrete poetry is closely related to the activities of the graphic artist, the typographer, and the advertising copy-writer. While concrete poetry is not an entirely modern movement (well known early poets like George Herbert and Robert Herrick produced concrete poems), it has attracted considerable interest in the last few decades. Because concrete poetry foregrounds language, foregrounds the materiality of language, it precludes the common reading practice of regarding language as transparent, a window onto the "real" world, an expression of truth instead of a construction of "truth." Readers of a concrete poem are arrested by the language. Instead of passing quickly through the portal of the poem into the world, they are compelled to explore the mechanics, the relationships, and the operations of language.

The following concrete poem presents only a glimmer of the innovative and imaginative work done in this area.

The Computer's First Birthday Card
by Edwin Morgan

many returns happy
many turns happier
happy turns remain
happy remains turn
turns remain happy
turn happy remains
remains turn happy
mains return happy
happy mains return
main happy returns
main turns happier
happier main turns
happier many turns
many happier turns
many happier turns
many happier turns
er turns er turns ?
happy er er happy ?
er *error* er *check*   !
turn er pre turns !
many happy turners
+$?-†!=%0$^1/_2$^'*/£(]&
many gay whistlers
no no no no no no!
many gainsboroughs
stop   stop   stop   stp
happier   constables
010101010101010101
raise police pay p
ost early for chri
stmas watch forest
fires get well soo
n bon voyage KRRGK
many happy returns
eh? eh? eh? eh? eh? eh?

23

One of the most common expectations most readers bring to their experience of a poem is that a poem will have some significance. In other words, the poem is not just a random collection of letters and shapes. Readers assume that there is purpose in the configuration of letters, and they will expend effort in order to recuperate the significance of the poem. Even when a poem appears to be haphazard and indecipherable, it can be recuperated as a statement about haphazardness and indecipherability. Or at least as wit and keen fun. Because Morgan's poem plays with the idea that the computer can randomly produce whatever words it chooses, and can get muddled about its objective (is it producing a birthday card or a message of a different kind?), and does this by substituting words that are close to but different from those which would achieve its objectives, it forces the reader to pay attention to how words mean and how their meaning can be "turned."

Questions to ask about Morgan's "The Computer's First Birthday Card" include, What are the effects of repeating and switching the words "many," "returns," and "happy," in the first part of the poem? What happens to the computer? What are the references to "turners," "whistlers," "gainsboroughs," and "constables"? Once students have gained a sense of how words can be broken and reshaped to produce a concrete poem, they may want to produce concrete poems of their own (an exercise which will, in turn, further their understanding of how concrete poems work). Here are some suggestions for producing concrete poems with your students.

ACTIVITY
Construct a poem using pairs of words such as, "you" and "I," "love" and "hate," "yes" and "no."

ACTIVITY
Construct a poem made up entirely of headlines and product labels cut out of newspapers and magazines. The poem can focus on a particular theme such as ecology, violence, or love.

ACTIVITY
Using the letters of the alphabet, different colours, illustrations, and im-

ages, construct a poem that looks like one of the following:

a donut
a flower
the wind
a cloud
the colour red
falling with a parachute
falling without a parachute
the world seen upside down
a rock
a report card

ACTIVITY
Construct a poem using just one vowel, as in the following example:

Point of View
by Carl Leggo

IIIIIIIII
IIIIIIII
IIIIIII
IIIIIII
IIIIII
IIIII
IIII
III
II
I

Sound Poems

Where concrete poems foreground the iconic materiality of language, sound poems foreground the aural materiality of language. Concrete and sound poems, then, remind us that language is a system of signs by drawing our attention to the signifiers, to the ways that the words are organized to create certain effects. Most of the time we use language without much awareness of the complicated strategies and devices and rules that produce the effects of meaning and understanding we experience from our reading. Most use of language foregrounds meaning and is designed to explain, persuade, and narrate—to reveal the world. Hence, language is standardized: news announcers sound the same, news magazine reporters write the same, textbooks imitate a textbook language, film stars imitate a film-star language. Teachers encourage their students to excise the idiosyncratic from their writing and to pursue the goals of unity, coherence, and emphasis so that their writing does not call attention to itself and is standardized, uniform, and predictable. Even much contemporary poetry effaces the materiality of the signifier. As a result students are isolated from one of the most distinctive qualities of language—its playfulness. As children grow up, they are delighted by nursery rhymes, skipping songs, and nonsense verse. They revel in the sounds generated by word play. David Hurry notes that children are instructed "how to mean successfully in society" by effacing "the childish fascination with the signifiers. Sound is increasingly discouraged as a significant (!) pleasure." (Hurry, 1986, 19) Yet there is no reason why that pleasure must end in adolescence or adulthood. Sound poems remind us to pay attention to the play of language.

The following poem, "Mountain Boogie," is a poem for reading aloud—for shouting, whispering, screaming, for rolling the tongue and the lips around, for wallowing in the lushness of oral language.

Mountain Boogie
by Peter van Toorn

O peppermint moon behind the loud running clouds!
O aspirin violets!
O the cue to look up splickering out there in the U-sphere!
O aspirin ivories!
O nick nock of madder smoosh!
O the sparks when she peels her sweater in the dark!
O sepia blush!
O pink pink: the fingers' rinks winking with quick!
O no go zipper zinc!
O comet locked up in the shed by mistake!

O the worm in the wick of the fire!
O that sienna stays!
O baby's milkteeth loose in a hailstorm!
O bright-assed baboon who sat on the peacock's glory!
O blue pencils of rain on the rooftiles!
O leapfrog green!
O mouse on the telephone: dunk your biscuit static!
O tapioca from Oka tango!
O chrome shimmy of blackfly blood!
O dill to pistachio!
O trout with a rainbow up, lungs two feet deep in sharp air!
O tobaggo nutmegs!
O angel hairs tuned in a cigarbox: *voilà! le clavecin!*
O tiny chrome haypiles of the stars!
O calico cat with the spaghetti whiskers!
O blizzard whites!
O piano crates unloading: thunder over Chinatown!
O old plum tree with the joker of jade up your sleeves!
O peonies! the flutes of spice!
O spinach wrinkles!
O fire chopping a log to stips of ash!
O yoghurt thwop!
O clam-shell tulip-cheeks!
O pink-spoggled eggs on umber craterboard!
O saffron velleity!
O opal winter lightning through the onyx glass!
O bamboo arpeggio!
O magnolia stalled like creamy brookwater!
O icicle pearls!
O for some steamy silvers to kick the goop out of flamingo balls!
O mustard glush!
O coffee, khaki, cookie, banana!
O peachy rhum goo!
O sunladder yellow!
O amber hoofclick!
O cowlick of cobalt left in for the last failing argument!
O ozone manure!
O lake red with gold-ishings in it!

27

O bronze leaf hopping a highway of mint & toffee headlights!
O cigarette paper rolled by fog tongue!
O crumpled copper onionwrap!
O perfume of the stars around the moon!
O barnstraw blond!
O lollipop lick of streaming tangerine air!

Some readers might want to analyze and explain "Mountain Boogie," to recuperate its meaning, to make it make sense. But its meaning lies in the way it invites readers to engage with the sense of hearing. One of the main qualities of "Mountain Boogie" is the way that the poet juxtaposes images that do not ordinarily go together ("worm in the wick of the fire" and "ozone manure"), makes up words ("splickering," "smoosh"), and repeats "O" and exclamation points. Hopefully, in response to it, students will want not just to write a poem but to write a sound poem. You could offer your students these suggestions for producing sound poems.

ACTIVITY

Produce a variant on Eugen Gomringer's famous "ping pong" poem or a poem, like his, based on a mere two words. Divide the class into groups of four or five students. Announce that each group is going to write a poem using just two words and then perform the poem orally. Here is Eugen Gomringer's poem:

ping pong
    ping pong ping
    pong ping pong
        ping pong

Students will likely produce equally innovative and striking poems.

ACTIVITY

Have your students choose a sound, any sound, and produce a poem from it. Some suggestions for noisy scenes or objects that might yield sound poems include a busy city street, the kitchen during breakfast, a snowstorm, clocks, and sleep (trying to get to sleep, falling asleep, dreaming, snoring, and coming out of sleep). A sound poem can be produced even from sounds that are simple and repetitive. Here is a poem I wrote about the sounds a Newfoundland fishing boat with a double-cylinder Acadia engine makes as it pulls out of the harbour:

Put Put
by Carl Leggo

> put put put put put put put put
> FUMP fump FUMP fump FUMP fump FUMP
> shash splu shash splu shash splu
> splu shash splu shash splu shash
> sous LLOP sous LLOP sous LLOP sous
> llop SOUS llop SOUS llop SOUS llop
> nat nat nat nat nat nat nat nat nat

ACTIVITY

Your students could take a completely different tack by producing a poem that is not based upon a particular sound or sounds but which produces its sonorousness from its own words. Read the following poem as well as the poet's explanation of his objectives in the poem:

Silent Poem
by Robert Francis

backroad leafmold stonewall chipmunk
underbrush grapevine woodchuck shadblow

woodsmoke cowbarn honeysuckle woodpile
sawhorse bucksaw outhouse wellsweep

backdoor flagstone bulkhead buttermilk
candlestick ragrug firedog brownbread

hilltop outcrop cowbell buttercup
whetstone thunderstorm pitchfork steeplebush

gristmill millstone cornmeal waterwheel
watercress buckwheat firefly jewelweed

gravestone groundpine windbreak bedrock
weathercock snowfall starlight cockcrow

About "Silent Poem" Francis observes:

> A fascination with words, single words or groups of words,
> has been the origin of a number of my recent poems. I be-
> came so fond of the strong character of solid compounds
> ("backroad," "stonewall," etc.) that I made a list purely for my
> pleasure. In time I wanted to make a poem out of these words,
> fitting them together like a patchwork quilt. In so doing I saw
> I could paint a picture of old-time New England, a picture
> moving from wildwood to dwelling, outdoors and in, then
> out and up to pasture and down to millstream. (Francis, 1977,
> 100)

By combining words in this way, Francis mimics the operation of
all poetry, which is a collage of sounds and sights. After examining "Silent Poem" students might enjoy writing a similar poem, perhaps about
some of the products or machines we use on a typical day or about the
seasons or school or war or the heavens.

The question, What is a poem? is a question that teachers and students need to ask continually as they read poetry together. There is no
simple answer, and the many possible answers will depend on the personal responses of readers. By reading a wide range of poems, students
will expand their expectations of what a poem is. They will more effectively attend to the many elements that can comprise poetry, such as
images, sounds, shapes, and themes, as well as develop a keener appreciation for the ways in which poets experiment and play with language,
tradition, and form. In the following theoretical section, I discuss reader-
response theory in order to lay a foundation for several approaches to
reading poetry that I have found to be successful in engaging students in
productive experiences with poems.

CHAPTER 2

Reader Response

My experiences as a student and teacher of English literature have been fairly diverse. As a student, I was required to memorize biographical sketches of authors, identify the source of selected quotations, scan lines, and label all examples of alliteration, simile, and apostrophe. As a teacher, I sent students into poems hunting for imagery and meaning. With hindsight I question whether perhaps I was like the father who told his daughter that she could go swimming, but that she must not go near the water. Too often my lessons were repetitive and superficial. I suspect I was afraid to lead my students too deeply into the text out of a fear that they would be lost, or would weary on the journey. I stuck with basic approaches, and if they did not really work, then at least the days passed fairly quickly and the poetry unit did not last forever.

From my experiences and observations as a poet and a teacher, I think that much poetry instruction is ineffectual because many teachers and students have, at best, an obscure definition of where they are going and an inadequate means for getting there. I am proposing an approach to poetry instruction that engages the reader with the text in a power struggle, not so much a struggle for the acquisition of power (although any encounter with language produces power), but an earnest endeavour to generate textual power. By textual power I mean the ways that language discloses and constructs the world for writers and readers. We write, read, think, talk, listen, represent, and know ourselves and others through language. When I read a poem, I bring experiences of language into connection with the language of the poetic text and with the language experiences of the poet and the whole cultural enterprise of poetry, and in these connections there is a dynamic dialogue. I learn about myself, and I learn about others, and I learn about the world, all through words. That is textual power, but for that power to be activated, I must be willing to devote attention to the dialogic connections between words, myself, and others. The production of textual power is hard work. It demands concentration, reflexivity, mental acuity, wide-ranging knowledge, confidence, and diffidence.

In basic terms, the reader-response approach I propose begins with the larger canvas—the general impression or experience of the poem. First, students hear and read the poem and write initial responses. Writing the responses is important because it gives students a chance to articulate reactions that are still mostly unformed, and because their written texts are now additional texts to be engaged in the discussion. The important realization at this stage is that students are not searching for a meaning. They are involved in a process of producing meaning out of their own reactions. There follows a further time of reflection and writing. Students then share their written texts with the texts of two or three others in their class. Next they articulate still further responses to the poem. What is the student responding to in the poem? The answer is anything: the shape of the poem, the stanzaic structure, the use of punctuation and capitalization, the length of the lines, the title, the spatial gaps, the words (known and unknown), relationships to personal experiences, intertextual references, the music, pictures of the imagination, the emotions, the characters, and/or the narratives.

But students need direction in what to look for. They cannot just be instructed to observe the landscape and describe it. They need opportunities to develop methods of discrimination. These opportunities can best be provided in the ongoing interaction of students and teachers with texts and with one another. Nobody has all the answers. A genuine process of inquiry is undertaken. Literary competence is developed through this process. Concepts are formulated through the experience of responding to poetry and sharing with the responses of others.

Unlike the New Critical approach that divorced the poem from its authorial, historical, and social contexts to examine its structure and reveal its unified meaning, the reader-response approach recognizes that a poem may have multiple meanings. Contexts—the author's and the reader's—are inseparably related to the poem; different readers may arrive at different meanings, and the same reader might arrive at different meanings at different times. In other words, author, text, and reader are integrally connected in the experience of a poem. Teachers are the facilitators leading their students to innovative ways of understanding. The growth in comprehension depends on the process of inquiry and discussion—the interaction (exploration, frustration, joy, argument, sharing, more exploration) among a group of readers with different personalities and backgrounds, different levels of literary competence, and different degrees of commitment to the poetic experience.

Perhaps the most significant disadvantage of the New Criticism is that by concentrating attention on how the machinery of the text (ambiguity, symbolism, paradox) produces the unitary meaning, the New Critics devalued the role of readers, who became functions of the text manipulated by the text to respond in certain ways. Readers were either competent or incompetent, depending on how successfully they were able to decode the poem and uncover its hidden meaning. As a consequence, the reader's responses are always governed by the dictates of the text. The value of the reader-response orientation lies in its recognition of the reader as active. Louise Rosenblatt, a pioneer in the debate about the role of the reader, explains: "The reading of a text is an event occurring at a particular time in a particular environment at a particular moment in the life history of the reader. The transaction will involve not only the past experience but also the present state and present interests or preoccupations of the reader."(Rosenblatt, 1978, 20) For Rosenblatt, the "text" is only "a set or series of signs interpretable as linguistic symbols." (12) The "poem," on the other hand, is "the experience shaped by the reader under the guidance of the text." (12) In other words, the poem is produced through the transaction between the reader and the text. I especially like Rosenblatt's suggestion that the reader is a performer impressing his or her own individuality upon a unique production or evocation of the poem. (28)

Not everybody committed to the reader-response orientation agrees with Rosenblatt concerning the transaction between the text and the reader. In *Is There a Text in This Class?*, Stanley Fish argues in favour of dismissing the tension between text and reader:

The entities that were once seen as competing for the right to constrain interpretation (text, reader, author) are now all seen to be the products of interpretation. A polemic that was mounted in the name of the reader and against the text has ended by the subsuming of both the text and reader under the larger category of interpretation. (Fish, 1980,17)

Fish contends that words have meanings because they are embedded in contexts. Consider the plurality of meanings generated by the expression, "I love you." The expression signifies different meanings in different contexts: a father to his child, a wife to her husband, a religious believer to God. What is pertinent is that people understand the different meanings intended in different contexts. Fish explains:

Communication occurs within situations and . . . to be in a situation is already to be in possession of (or to be possessed by) a structure of assumptions, of practices understood to be relevant in relation to purposes and goals that are already in place; and it is within the assumption of these purposes and goals that any utterance is immediately heard. (318)

For Fish, then, readers and authors and texts are inextricably wedded to systems of intelligibility and interpretive communities.

Without question, Fish's proposal provides a useful perspective on the relationship between the text and the reader, but his suggestion that both the text and the reader are subsumed under the larger category of interpretation does not deny that the reader and the text both have active roles to perform in the reading process. Readers and authors can choose to disrupt and expand systems of intelligibility and can refuse to obey interpretive constraints. A notable weakness of Fish's proposal is that it posits a super-reader who is well informed about interpretive conventions and constraints. Since few readers (and even fewer adolescent readers) meet the mark of Fish's ideal reader, a theory of reading needs to address the perspective and understanding of ordinary readers. Even while agreeing that meaning is determined by interpretive contexts, that meaning is still produced by the interactive participation of a reader and a text. Rather than suggest that reader and text are subsumed by the larger category of interpretation, let us suggest that readers are empowered or guided by interpretive contexts.

Also well known for his reader-response orientation is David Bleich, who emphasizes the role of the reader's personality and experience. Bleich argues for "subjective criticism" which entails the exploration of emotional responses. Bleich is far less interested in the constraints of the text. For him the text is really a starting point for the articulation of the reader's lived experience. Bleich is particularly relevant for issues of pedagogy because he contends that relationships "between student and student and between teacher and student" need to operate on the basis of open, honest sharing. (Bleich, 1980, 159) He recognizes that critics of his view are convinced that "any means of making subjective experiences public necessarily leads to psychological danger, intellectual disarray, and pedagogical anarchy," but he defends his approach with the general rejoinder that "such pitfalls are the common risks of any social initiative that involves new thinking." (158)

Even though Rosenblatt, Fish, and Bleich all fall under the rubric of reader-response criticism, there are obvious and important differences among them. For the teacher of secondary English, their innovative contributions to literary theory are inestimably useful because they open up a broad range of opportunities for new ways of reading and responding to literature. New Criticism's rigorous attention to the text was a necessary and welcome alternative to a concentration on the biography and the intention of the author, but to emphasize the role of the text ("the verbal icon") is to view the reading process too narrowly.

Reader-response theorists provide a needed remedy for the revitalization of literary study. Nevertheless, I have some reservations about reader-response approaches. Fish is instructive, but he limits the role of the reader, and Bleich undermines the role of the text by emphasizing the personal or subjective response. As much as I admire Bleich's vision of an environment where open, honest sharing is activated, the typical school classroom is hardly designed or intended for group therapy. Bleich does not provide a sufficiently comprehensive or workable strategy for the classroom. Herein lies my principal reservation about the reader-response orientation: the onus of responsibility for producing a "poem" out of a "text" rests on the shoulders of an adolescent reader. Teachers might not like to admit the realization I once painfully arrived at: students do not know a great many things. It is futile (destructive even) to expect students to articulate personal responses to every text. A personal response can hardly be commanded. Moreover, the articulation of personal responses is only one part of schooling whose larger goal is equipping students with the confidence and the skills to engage in the life-long articulation of personal responses. And that is why I think Rosenblatt provides indispensable advice for reading poetry: she recognizes a balance between the text and the reader. On the one hand, the reader's personality, emotions, and experiences are all called into active participation with the text. On the other hand, the text is a system of signs that helps guide the reader's response. In this way, both the subjective and the objective aspects of the reading process are married.

The progeny of this marriage is a wide-ranging perspective on poetry reading. Instead of restricting the term "reader response" to the ideas of a select few, teachers can expand the use of the term to include a broad, eclectic mixture of strategies for reading and responding to poetry. An emotional response is only one kind of response, as is a response that pays attention only to the technical devices of a poem, or to its meaning, or to its relation to history. Teachers can combine New Criticism's emphasis on careful attending to the text of a poem with the focus of reader-response theorists on the wide-ranging possibilities for interpreting a poem.

The typical poetry lesson in secondary school is directed towards the production of a critical analysis paper. A cursory review of the kinds of questions asked in school textbooks is adequate to prove that the overriding purpose of reading poetry is to identify theme, metre, figurative speech, rhyme, imagery, design, and symbolism. Having identified the elusive creatures lying hidden behind the black marks on the page, it is a relatively easy procedure to pass judgment on the author's effective use of the tools of his or her trade. The critical analysis paper attempts to excavate the poem, to force it into a single perspective, and to close down the subject. It is interested only in the final product, a coherent, unified explanation of the way the parts of the poem are interrelated. Any inconsistency, incoherence, gaps, undecidability in language and meaning will be ironed out or ignored. How many grade nine students really enjoy answering the following questions about Shakespeare's "Sonnet XXX" from *Searchlights* (1970, 1:8)?

1. Show that the form of the Elizabethan or Shakespearean sonnet is suitable for the development of the poet's ideas.
2. The sonnet is a poetic form in which the ideas are expressed in very compact form. Prove that "Sonnet XXX" gives evidence of this concept.
3. Pick out two metaphors which are effectively expressed, and explain why the poet has used each of these.

This kind of approach to reading poetry guarantees that most students will develop an inveterate antipathy for poetry (at least the kind of poetry they meet in school). They might still enjoy the lyrics of contemporary music, the poetry of advertising, stand-up comics, and Hallmark cards, and even the occasional Yeats poem quoted in a television hospital drama, but they will harbour a life-long distaste for reading poetry.

In the classroom, the reader's transaction with the text must be the focus of critical attention. Any initial response by a reader—disgust or frustration or awe (Yuck! Dense! Wow!)—is a valuable starting point for a progressive encounter with the text. Students need to be given opportunities to express their responses orally and in writing, and to revise and share them. Teachers, too, need to engage in a transaction with the text, and produce their performances of poems for their students.

The reader-response orientation is not for teachers and students who are faint-hearted. It is unpredictable and demanding. It encourages reflexivity and sharing. It does not lend itself to objective evaluation. (Teachers, if they must evaluate, will especially need to evaluate effort.) It contributes to a classroom environment full of noise and energy (not always conducive to harmony with the administration). It is not easy to teach—in fact, perhaps it cannot be taught. Instead teachers might have to be content with providing opportunities for growing and learning. They ought to examine ways to facilitate student responses. Teachers might introduce each lesson with a bold manifesto: Let's struggle with a poem. Let's express the struggle. Let's talk and write reflexively. Let's perform the text. Let's allow the text to work us over and let us work the text over. The experience of reading poetry this way will encourage students and teachers (at least some) to be energetic and imaginative performers of texts. The approaches to reading poetry which follow in the next four

37

sections are designed to guide teachers and students as they begin using a reader-response orientation.

Problem Makers

One of the most prevalent weaknesses of students' responses to poetry is the persistent tendency to closure. Patrick Dias describes four kinds of readers: paraphrasers, thematizers, allegorizers, and problem solvers. Paraphrasers seldom push "beyond the literal meaning of the poem." (Dias, 1986, 46) Thematizers seek to "crack the code" of the poem and conceptualize a general theme about "Life, Nature, Man, Animals, Landscapes, or Loneliness." (47) Allegorizers are intent on exercising ingenuity "to work out the equivalences between the poem and life," (48) even if their ingenuity requires twisting "the text to fit the meaning they are creating." (49) According to Dias, paraphrasers, thematizers, and allegorizers are ineffective readers because they are all motivated by the desire to consume the poem, to close off the encounter with the text. Problem solvers, on the other hand, refuse "to settle immediately on meaning" and are "tentative in their formulations of meaning" (49) because "for them, a poem is never ever fully understood." (50)

Needed are reading strategies that defer closure and promote openness in the encounter with poems. While I applaud Dias's research and insights, I question his term "problem solvers" because it still suggests that a poem is a puzzle that can be solved and closed. I prefer the label "problem makers" because it implies a refusal to invite closure. I recommend an approach to reading a poem which treats the poem as an expansive space to romp and play in, to explore and travel in. The responsive reader is a problem maker. In order to help readers become more responsive, more willing to engage in a performance of the poem, teachers must encourage students to spend time with the poem. One way to foster reading as problem making is to invite readers to pose their initial responses in the form of questions which do not need to be ordered or categorized. Instead of expressing their interaction with a poem in declarative sentences which posit statements and conclusions (however inconclusive), readers can compile a lengthy and wide-ranging list of questions generated by reading and rereading the poem.

Problem Making in the Classroom

During the school year 1989 to 1990, I taught English at Herdman Collegiate in Corner Brook, Newfoundland. For several lessons I invited my students to respond with questions to several of my poems. One lesson focused on the following poem:

I Still Hear the Bell Ringing
by Carl Leggo

On long walks from Crescent Pond
in cool/warm Mays on the keen edge
of promised summer (our creels
heavy with a dozen trout more
than the law permitted) my father
offered the only advice I remember:

    Take your garbage home,
and in my knapsack, then and now,
empty Vienna sausage cans,
wax paper, pop bottles

    If you don't know a word,
      look it up in a dictionary,
strong advice, for now I know
many words and in words I am known

    Never hate anybody,
wisdom like an iron bell ringing
from a gray sky, its echoes
heard through the years

   Never hate anybody
      Never hate anybody
My one wish (who needs three?):
on long walks from Crescent Pond
through the dense spruce, across the bog

on a trail only my father could see,
I wish he had taught me how

After I read the poem to the students, I asked them to respond to it with questions. I advised them to ask questions about anything. I explained that the purpose of the exercise was to generate questions as paths into the poem, as ways to explore the significance of the poem. There was some initial confusion and hesitation: "Just ask questions? About anything? Are you sure?" But my students accepted the invitation and produced lists of questions that clearly indicated they were responding to the poem from many different perspectives. Some students had the sense that they were addressing their questions directly to me, but I warned my students that poets do not necessarily have the answers to questions generated by readers.

The following list of questions is a sample of the questions that my secondary students asked about "I Still Hear the Bell Ringing":

1.   What does the bell ringing have to do with the poem?
2.   How come you named the poem "I Still Hear the Bell Ringing" when it only refers to it once?
3.   Where is Crescent Pond?
4.   What does "our creels heavy with a dozen trout" mean?
5.   How come at one point you're talking about fish and garbage and then turn around and start talking about words in dictionaries?
6.   What does "in words I am known" mean?
7.   How come you say "never hate anybody" twice together?
8.   Was this poem really about your father taking you on fishing trips?
9.   What do you wish your father had taught you?
10. Is your father dead, or did you just put the poem in the past tense?
11. What do you mean when you say "take your garbage home, then and now"?
12. How come you wrote the poem in the way it's written?
13. Was Crescent Pond far from civilization?
14. What does "wisdom like an iron bell ringing" mean?
15. Why did you divide cool and warm with a "/"?
16. Why would your father let you take more fish than the law permitted?

17. Was that the only advice your father gave you?
18. Was Crescent Pond surrounded by a forest or just some trees?
19. Was it only you that your father took fishing?
20. How does a dictionary give "strong advice"?
21. Is it legal to trout that early in the year?
22. What does "on the keen edge" mean?
23. Would the bell act as a guide to people (or you) further in life?
24. Why would your father tell you to take home garbage? Wouldn't you have enough sense to do it anyway?
25. Why is this poem one long sentence?
26. Why does he refer to the father's wisdom as a ringing iron bell?
27. What does wisdom have to do with an iron bell?
28. Why did you use brackets in this poem?
29. Why is the poem written in this shape and with this arrangement?
30. What bell is the writer hearing ring?
31. How can you walk "on the keen edge of promised summer"?
32. How old is the writer in the poem?
33. What are creels?
34. What is the setting of the poem?
35. Who is the speaker?
36. How do the stanzas relate to one another?
37. Is this a true story?
38. What are "cool/warm Mays"?
39. Does the son receive all the advice at once?
40. Why don't you have a period at the end?
41. Why did you indent the first two lines in the third paragraph?
42. How come his father was the only one who could see the trail?
43. Why did you exceed the trout limit?
44. What does the author wish his father had taught him how to do?
45. What is the father like?
46. How much time has passed since the words of advice were given?
47. Why did you use colons?
48. Who is the "I" in the poem?
49. Does the trail symbolize something? Does the trail have a meaning?
50. Why did the poet ask only one wish and not three?

51. What is the theme of the poem?
52. Why is the sky gray and not blue?
53. Where did the author get the similes (like an iron bell)?
54. Why did you write this poem?
55. Why doesn't this poem rhyme?

Students concurred that this approach was non-threatening, even fun. Many of them expressed surprise at how many questions they asked. Semantic, syntactic, and prosodic questions were intermingled with personal and reflective questions. Some students spoke about the sense of freedom that they enjoyed during the process of questioning. They did not feel any pressure to produce the correct answers. One student observed, "With each new question I felt like I was opening up another window on the poem."

After compiling the list of questions, my students and I confronted the issue of what to do with them and decided to do nothing. Too many students grow up with the mistaken notion that all questions have answers and that questions are meant to be answered. The advantages of doing nothing with the questions are multiple: the poem remains open, the questions hint at tantalizing ideas, experiences, people, and places to pursue, and the questioner remains open.

Students will eventually engage in more definite responses. But as an initial strategy for encouraging an active participation with a text, the exercise of posing questions without seeking conclusions motivates more readers to be problem makers.

Responding Out Loud

A reader-response orientation to reading poetry can be threatening because it is unpredictable. The teacher cannot begin the class with a meticulously prepared lesson plan detailing objectives, activities, and exercises in neatly apportioned allotments of time. The teacher is not armed with eight comprehension questions to be answered, a guidebook with the correct answers, and a red pencil to indicate all ill-founded suggestions from students. As Robert E. Probst recommends, "the pattern of questioning in response-based teaching begins with the most amorphous, non-directive question possible, something analogous to a shrug of the shoulders or a 'Well, what do you make of this?'" (Probst, 1984, 44)

Unfortunately, I've asked high school students that question and been met by an unnerving silence. But it isn't only the fear of silence which makes the reader-response orientation threatening. Teachers cannot predict what the students will say. They need to be astute like news reporters in probing, questioning, challenging, summarizing, and clarifying. Reading a poem and asking students to answer comprehension questions would be a less complicated, less risky approach to teaching a poem than an approach which invites a whole class to respond openly and out loud.

The following poem is one of my favourite poems for generating discussion in a class:

**th wundrfulness uv th mountees
our secret police**
by bill bissett

they opn our mail   petulantly
they burn down barns they cant
bug   they listn to our politikul
ledrs phone conversashuns   what
cud b less inspiring to ovrheer

they had me down on th floor til
i turnd purpul thn my frends
pulld them off me   they think
brest feeding is disgusting   evry
time we cum heer to raid ths place
yu always have that kid on yr   tit

they tore my daughtrs dolls hed off
looking for dope   whun uv my mor
memorabul beetings was in th back
seet lockd inside whun a ther unmarkd
cars

43

they work for th CIA   at nite they
drive around nd shine ther serchlites
on peopul embracing   nd with ther
p a systems tell them to keep away
from th treez

they listn to yr most secret farts
re-winding th tape looking for hiddn
meening   indigestyun is a nashunal
security risk

i think they shud stick to protecting
th weak   eldrly laydees n men childrn
crossing th street   helping sick
nd/or defensless peopul nd
arresting capitalist crooks

insted theyve desertid th poor
n eldrly   nd ar protecting
th capitalist crooks

its mor than musical
th ride theyr taking
us all on

     While I cannot predict the kinds of anecdotes and reactions and responses that bissett's poem will generate in a classroom, I am reasonably sure that the poem will not invite silence. A poem that castigates the police, uses words like "tit," "dope," and "farts," and misspells more words than Ralph who sits in the corner will almost certainly elicit vocal and abundant responses. The issue facing the teacher is how to deal with the responses generated by questions such as: Is bissett correct? Are the Royal Canadian Mounted Police as corrupt and oppressive as bissett contends? What have our personal experiences with the RCMP been? What are our attitudes to the RCMP? Why does bissett misspell words? What kind of person is the "i"? What is the effect of referring to the RCMP as "they"? Is the "i" raving? Credible? Reliable?

The pressing issue here is the right of students to hold opinions and to have the freedom to examine those opinions. bissett's poem is angry and vulgar. It is its boldness and crudity that open up perspectives for discussion. Some people will probably object to the use of this poem in a school poetry lesson and claim that it's too political, too inflammatory, too critical, too unbalanced, or too indelicate. But students will identify with it. They may respond with a measure of surprise that "th wundrfulness uv th mountees our secret police" is a poem.

After discussing bisset's poem with a class of grade ten students, I asked them how they felt about the issue of censorship in the classroom. Their replies reminded me that teachers need to be careful not to impose their own sense of what is appropriate literature for reading in the classroom, or what appropriate responses to literature are. As one student observed, "Every person is an individual with a unique personality who should have the right to express his or her views, and the classroom should give the chance for this." Another student suggested, "Everything should be talked about in class. If people talked about really deep subjects, there wouldn't be so much prejudice in the world."

When teachers invite students to respond to bissett's poem (or any poem) in class, they cannot control the responses. They might not like or agree with many of the responses, but they do not control the responses. They invite their students to talk, to express their views, to participate in a collaborative venture of exploring issues and making sense of their experiences in the world.

Responding to a Poem Subjectively

Reader-response theorists argue for the value of courting and encouraging subjective responses, but there is the danger that teachers subscribing to it may concentrate *only* on subjective responses. David Bleich's insistence on a subjective response that significantly ignores the text and focusses instead on the reader's emotions, experiences, and personality can lead to reading practices that fail to recognize the interactive relationship between the reader and the text. Deanne Bogdan criticizes

Bleich's emphasis on subjective response as "reading for feeling good" or "ego-massage," and argues instead for "a syncretic approach to literary response," one built on a combination of attention to subjective responses as well as "the very lifeblood of literature, its formal structure." (Bogdan, 1984, 71) Subsequent strategies in this book will address Bogdan's concerns, but in advocating the soliciting of subjective responses in the classroom, I want to stress the merits of a response which is shamelessly, deliberately personal and emotional. Such a response is only a partial response, but it can provide a basic and inviting way to begin reading poetry. In a subjective response, teachers are not specifically concerned with the use of stanzaic structure, imagery, punctuation, and allusions in a poem, nor are they proposing that a personal response to a poem is exhaustive. The subjective response is a first-step response that students can habitually engage in when reading poetry.

Eliciting Subjective Responses in the Classroom

As a teacher I like to model the approaches to reading poetry that I invite my students to use. The following illustration of responding to a poem subjectively indicates how I have used this approach with my students. I read "Mother" by Andrew Waterman and wrote a subjective response to it. I pretended I was writing a diary entry or a personal letter. Waterman's poem is about a son's memories of his experiences with his mother who often seemed distant and reserved. The poem begins with the following lines:

Mother
by Andrew Waterman

I should be grateful. You
adopted me in a hard time,
the sound of guns from Dunkirk shaking
London, the bombs. You have told
how once you lay over my pram as a German
aeroplane swooped to machine-gun the street.
What made you, you never did say.

46

Here is my subjective response to Waterman's poem:

Dear Mother,
There are so few memories: Mostly I remember your peeling
potatoes for French fries and getting tea for Dad and hanging out
the laundry (hands red in the white February air) and walking
through the city and the seasons (always fast like you had
somewhere to go) and posing in the new dress (your eyes filled with
eagerness for the New Year's Eve Dance). I can't remember if I
hugged you or kissed you. I remember wanting to, but not
knowing how.

I shared my subjective response with my students so they could see
how my response elicited specific memories. My subjective response raised
several emotional issues for me. Not all teachers will feel comfortable in
personal revelation, but teachers who invite their students to respond
subjectively to poems need to be prepared to do the same. For inviting
subjective responses to a poem, use poems that are readily accessible and
personal. Andrew Waterman's poem speaks about the parent-child relationship in ways with which many people can identify. The lyrics of contemporary songs provide a rich treasure of poetry for inviting subjective
responses. The goal of this initial approach is to help students understand that poetry is not an arcane and boring school exercise, but a way
of engaging with the heart, the mind, and the spirit of lived experiences.

Eliciting a Stream-of-Consciousness Response in the Classroom

Students need to be given ample opportunities as well as encouragement
to respond to poetry. In many classrooms the teacher is the pre-eminent
wordsmith revelling or wallowing in an endless stream of words about
his/her opinions, reactions, plans, conclusions. In order to elicit more
bountiful responses, the teacher can invite students to share their reactions to a poem in a stream-of-consciousness format. While reading and
rereading a poem, students are encouraged to write down impressions,
questions, connections, emotions, and anecdotes evoked by the poem.
In a stream-of-consciousness approach, readers record as many of their

reactions as they can in a prescribed period of time (say ten to twenty minutes). As they write their reactions, students should not concern themselves with the organization, structure, or grammar of their notes. Their goal is to generate words on paper. The following illustration of reading a poem in a stream-of-consciousness response demonstrates how open and wide-ranging this approach can be. By engaging in the process of a stream-of-consciousness response, teachers can help students understand how reading is a process of making meaning by recalling and reconsidering questions, memories, and insights.

ACTIVITY
Running on Empty
by Robert Phillips

As a teenager I would drive Father's
Chevrolet cross-county, given me

reluctantly: "Always keep the tank
half full, boy, half full, ya hear?"

The fuel gauge dipping, dipping
toward Empty, hitting Empty, then

–thrilling!–' way below Empty,
myself driving cross-county

mile after mile, faster and faster,
all night long, this crazy kid driving

the earth's rolling surface,
against all laws, defying chemistry,

rules, and time, riding on nothing
but fumes, pushing luck harder

than anyone pushed before, the wind
screaming past like the Furies . . .

I stranded myself only once, a white
night with no gas station open, ninety miles

from nowhere. Panicked for a while,
at standstill, myself stalled.

At dawn the car and I both refilled. But,
Father, I am running on empty still.

     I wrote the following notes in my own ten-minute stream-of-consciousness response:

— I know this teenager.
— It's wonderful to take risks, to be reckless.
— A father is full of strong advice, but who wants to live like a father.
— Am I really willing to be reckless?
— I like the way I can see the fuel gauge dipping, dipping towards empty, below empty I can feel the keen thrill of fear and risk.
— Why do poets always draw an important analogy between an event and life?
— The Furies refer to Greek mythology I'd like to know more about them.
— My father wouldn't teach me to drive too scared I think.
— Two-line stanzas help increase the speed of the poem I can feel and hear the speed stanzas three to six are all one long breathless sentence then in stanza seven a new sentence begins and the speaker is stranded. The several short sentences give the feeling of being stranded.
— I like the use of "ya" and "'way."
— What is "a white night" like?
— Is running on empty the best way to run?
— What would happen if we all ran on empty?
— Can we ever escape laws, chemistry, rules, and time?
— My brother Rick was reckless did lots of crazy things beat himself up

almost got killed once or twice.
— I seem to admire risk-taking, but I never take any I should have been
a banker.
— What does the speaker mean when he says both he and the car are
refilled? The car is filled with gas, of course, but what is the speaker
filled with breakfast, fresh resolve, even more courage for recklessness?
— Was he really "pushing luck harder than anyone pushed before"?
There doesn't seem to have been that much danger in his escapades.
— What was the big deal? Something like a harmless game of Russian
roulette without grave consequences.
— The car and the driver seem united he speaks of himself as "stalled,"
not the car.
— What does "running on empty still" mean?
— The tone is the boastful, taunting attitude of a daredevil, but is he
really a daredevil?
— Who is the speaker addressing? He speaks to his father at the end,
but the first part is not addressed to the father.
— The repetition of words ("dipping, dipping," "faster and faster")
produces the impression of speed. Why? How is that effect created?
Could I read this poem slowly?

Students can be provided both with Phillips' poem and the above
stream-of-consciousness response as long as they do not find my stream-
of-consciousness response constraining. Students need to be encouraged
to jot down notes without having to impress anybody. Stream-of-consciousness responses should be haphazard, unpredictable, and unstruc-
tured encounters with the text of the poem. While readers are intent on
responding and making meaning, the process is often not orderly, and
students should feel free to provide significantly personal and idiosyncratic responses.

ACTIVITY

In a typical classroom there are always some students who lack the confidence to share their responses in the open forum of the whole class. An
open forum means that only a few people will get much time to contribute. Therefore, after students write their stream-of-consciousness entries

in a poetry response journal, I suggest that you have them form pairs to share their responses. The task of the four-person groups is to select two comments and two questions. The groups should then pair and select one comment and one question for presentation to the entire class. Clearly there are dangers inherent in this approach. Since the small group discussions are mostly undirected by the teacher, there is always the possibility that students will discuss last night's hockey game or what's happening to Mitch and Becky on the soap operas. Nevertheless, students need to be given opportunities to grow as independent learners willing to take responsibility for their education.

Mike Hayhoe, who has used a method related to this approach, comments:

> The advantages of this method's occasional use are several: extended dwelling with a poem; collaborative enquiry; the direct use of language to explore language; the production and testing of an agenda through increasingly public groupings. For the teacher, there is a chance to be a genuine observer and to enquire into how his or her students make meaning from a poem. Finally, the technique does not leave a poem "solved" and done with. (Hayhoe, 1984, 42-43)

Obviously, this approach is closely related to the previous three approaches, "Problem Makers," "Responding Out Loud," and "Responding to a Poem Subjectively." I have used these approaches in my classes as orientation or warm-up activities in order to lure students into productive encounters with poems by helping them realize that poetry is relevant to their lives.

After students have experienced several poems using these orientation approaches, they will be ready to read poems with careful attention to the ways a poem works as a text. To guide them, the theoretical perspective of semiotics will help.

CHAPTER 3

Semiotics

While I recommend the merits of reader-response approaches for reading and teaching poetry, students need more than an invitation to respond personally to poems. The reader-response orientation establishes a perspective on the relationship between readers and texts, but for that relationship to be productive, readers need knowledge and skills to guide and inform them in their engagement with texts. The pressing question is, How can the reader engage in the reading process in a way that leads to the production of complex emotional and intellectual responses?

Readers need to know the conventions, codes, and rules of poetry. But efforts to establish rules for poetry often prove to be inadequate. In a recent poetry workshop for teachers a participant said, "I always thought that the first letter in each line of a poem had to be capitalized." While it is true that there is a long tradition of beginning each line of a poem with a capital, this is at best a description of a specific practice, not a prescription for general or necessary practice. It is not possible to establish a set of rules that will account for all the effects poets achieve in their poetry. A textbook like *A Prosody Handbook* by Karl Shapiro and Robert Beum is a valuable resource for guiding a reader of poetry. It provides useful terminology and informs readers about elements of poetry to pay attention to, but it cannot be regarded as definitive because there are so many exceptions to its rules in poetic practice. Traditional poetics is especially ineffective for reading much modern poetry, in particular experimental poetry. Knowing how to identify different kinds of regular rhythm will not be useful for reading contemporary poetry because most modern poetry is blatantly irregular.

Semiotics helps. In *Messages and Meanings: An Introduction to Semi-*

otics, Marcel Danesi explains that "semiotics teaches us how to read or interpret the meaning inherent in any human-made message or artifact. It is the 'science of messages and meanings' and of the signs and codes we use to produce and understand them." (Danesi, 1994, 2) According to semiotics, a poem is a network of signs that can be interpreted as meaningful because the signs are part of specific contexts and codes that readers understand as conventionally characteristic of poetry. Consider the following found poem:

San Francisco
by Richard Brautigan

By accident, you put
Your money in my
Machine (#4)
By accident, I put
My money in another
Machine (#6)
On purpose, I put
Your clothes in the
Empty machine full
Of water and no
Clothes

It was lonely.

(This poem was found written on a paper bag in a laundromat in San Francisco.)

What are the signs that invite a person to read "San Francisco" as a poem? What makes this collection of words a poem? First of all, the words are arranged in a pattern that establishes certain expectations. "San Francisco" looks like a poem. Each line begins with a capital; the standard rules of punctuation are not used; the text is divided into two stanzas; a title is given; the first three lines are repeated with variation in the next three lines, creating a musical effect; lines seven to eleven build on the

pattern of the first six lines but set up a contrast which leads to the con-
cluding line. Moreover, even though the poem is made up of simple words
and simple syntactic structures, its meaning is not simple. A bigger story
is hinted at. Is the empty machine that the narrator has put the clothes in
the same machine (#6) that he or she accidentally put the money in? The
poem is like the description in the ninth line, "Empty machine full." For
example, what does "it" refer to in the final line ("It was lonely")? Does
"it" refer to the empty machine, or to the situation of the narrator who is
alone in the laundromat and making decisions about what to do with
the mix-up of machines? What is the effect of setting off the final line
("It was lonely") as a separate stanza?

Semiotics is derived in significant ways from the linguistic struc-
turalism of Ferdinand de Saussure, who proposed that language is com-
prised of both *langue*–the structure of language, and *parole*–the practice
of language in specific contexts. Saussure focussed his attention on *langue*,
and semiotic approaches to reading focus on the structures, codes, and
conventions of literature. As a consequence, many semiotic approaches
to reading literature have been rejected as inadequate and even counter-
productive. But Robert Scholes defends a semiotic approach that incorporates both langue and parole, an approach that invites readers to linger with the poetic text in and for itself while acknowledging that the
text is part of larger contexts, including the context of the reader's phe-
nomenal world and the context of the world in which literature is read
and transmitted.

What does semiotics offer to secondary school students to help them
read poetry with more satisfaction and success? Semiotics demystifies
the misconception students have of poetry as inaccessible by suggesting
that, as a network of signs, a poem is something they can learn to read
much as they would learn to read any sign system (say traffic signs). Bor-
rowing from Northrop Frye, I call the signs of poetry "babble" and "doodle." If a poem is regarded as a textual weaving of signs, "babble" refers to
those signs which are primarily aural and appeal to the sense of hearing,
such as rhyme, rhythm, onomatopoeia, cadence, and alliteration, while
"doodle" refers to those signs which are primarily visual and appeal to
the sense of sight, such as imagery, similes, metaphors, figurative language, layout on the page, shape, and stanzaic structure. The more knowl-

edge a reader has of the many signs that comprise poetry, the more readily the reader can make meaning out of the poetic text.

But knowledge of the many signs that comprise a poem is no guarantee that a reader will respond to a poem with satisfaction or success. Knowing what an oxymoron is and identifying an oxymoron in a poem is no guarantee that the reader will interpret the use of the oxymoron in the context of the poem as significant for the meaning-making possibilities of the poem. Semiotics is not about labeling the parts of an artifact like a museum exhibit. Instead, semiotics facilitates readers' experiences of a poem by making readers more aware of the conventions of a poem so that their readings will be more receptive and perceptive. As the reader's comprehension of the conventions and the codes of poetry increases, the reader responds to poems with greater facility. Semiotics is valuable because it promotes both richer understanding and enhanced pleasure with its concentration on the reader's involvement with the effects of a poem and how those effects are achieved. Scholes provides a concise evaluation of the pertinence of semiotics: "A semiotic approach to poetry is neither vastly different from other effective approaches nor foolproof as a method. What it offers . . . is a methodology that is explicit, consistent, and therefore pedagogically useful as a way of developing interpretive flexibility and sensitivity in students of literature." (Scholes, 1982, 56)

Terry Eagleton criticizes semiotics because he claims that as an approach to reading poetry it requires a super-reader or ideal reader with exhaustive literary competence and knowledge, (Eagleton, 1983, 121) but semiotics is a broad discipline with a long history, and cannot be dismissed as easily as Eagleton wishes. While semiotics suggests that a reader needs knowledge of the codes and conventions of poetry, it also suggests that this knowledge will be developed in the process of reading poetry. Expressed in a simple way, semiotics reminds readers that texts are not empty vessels to be filled with any meaning nor are they mystically conjured texts with secret and indecipherable meanings.

In the following several sections readers are invited to respond to poetry semiotically by concentrating on the aural and visual signs, the babble and doodle, in poems.

Reading the Signs, Writing the Poem

Semiotics reminds us that one of the most common practices involved in reading a poem is to construct a narrative context for the poem. This practice is so common that many readers do it without being aware that they are actually constructing the situation. For example, it is typical to regard a poem, especially a lyric poem, as an utterance between a poet and a reader. Therefore, the narrating "I" of the poem is identified with the poet in an autobiographical connection that ignores and misses the simple fact that a poem is a verbal and rhetorical construct which invites many different responses from different readers. When I discussed reader-response approaches, I suggested several strategies that used the poem as a site for the reader to respond in blatantly personal and subjective ways. But the most useful reader-response approaches acknowledge the connections between the reader, the text, the author, and the social, political, and cultural contexts which inform and guide readers and texts and authors. Semiotics enhances the role of the text in the reading process, but semiotics does not neglect the reader's involvement or the author or the contexts in which readers, authors, and texts converge. In the next strategy I make use of the semiotic approach of creating a narrative context for the poetic text. Many semioticians would probably not agree with the way that I freely connect my personal experiences, memories, and prejudices to the poet's text. A semiotics approach begins with close attention to the text, to the way that the parts of the text relate to one another and to the larger contexts of generic expectations and conventions. But because I am seeking ways to connect reader-response approaches as traditionally practised in classrooms with the strategies of semiotics, I suggest using semiotics in idiosyncratic ways that will be useful for helping students read poetry.

Reading with Your Ears

How can the limited time available in secondary English classes be most effectively used to invite students to respond to the sounds of poems? Should students be taught how to scan lines, to identify regular metrical patterns, to label the repetition of consonants and vowels? While there is value in learning these skills, they can be effectively acquired, as needed, by readers who engage with poems in meaning-making responses. Moreover, students will need to know two terms for attending to the aural signifiers of a poem: consonance and rhythm. The term "consonance," which Don Gutteridge proposes "to refer to all types of meaningful repetition of consonants and vowels," (Gutteridge, 1983, 3) can adequately include alliteration, assonance, word repetition, rhyme, refrain, and onomatopoeia. Students might eventually learn definitions for all these terms and identify their specific use in poems, but instead of drilling students in the terms, I prefer to encourage them to be receptive to the repetition of sounds in poetry. The aural signifiers do not simply echo or embroider the meaning of the poem; they are integrally involved in the construction of the poem's semantic effects.

Similarly, instead of concentrating on various metrical patterns to describe rhythm (such as the syllabic, the accentual, or the accentual-syllabic including iambic pentameter), I prefer to explain rhythm by its relationship to speech. The rhythm of poetry is related to the rhythm of ordinary speech because both poetry and speech are characterized by stress patterns. By recognizing the kinship between the rhythm of poetry and the rhythm of ordinary speech, students can be encouraged to know that they already have the basic tools they need for responding to the rhythm of a poem. Randolph Quirk suggests helpfully:

> For all its artfulness and (sometimes strenuous) complexity, poetry is not disjunct from but intimately bedded in the most commonplace fundamentals of our everyday speech rhythm and grammar: even in the most everyday strategies of conversational discourse. (Quirk, 1982, v-vi)

Nevertheless, I do not want to equate the rhythm of poetry and the rhythm of ordinary speech because poetry is language that calls attention to itself. Derek Attridge explains:

> We grow accustomed to the speech we use and hear around us every day, and take for granted the easy passage from words to ideas; the strange, organized language of poetry deautomatises and defamiliarises that response, foregrounds the language itself rather than its subject, establishes a set towards the medium and not the message, and interrogates the

connections between sounds and meanings. (Attridge, 1982, 310-11)

Attridge questions "the assumption that verse is a representation of an individual's spoken words" and argues that "the value of metre lies in its capacity to render language unlike the language of daily communication, whether in its potency, its patterning, or its self-consciousness as a conventional system." (311-12) So, the rhythm of poetry is both similar and dissimilar to the rhythm of speech. It differs from the rhythm of ordinary language because it draws attention to itself as a signifying system.

Equipped with the concepts of consonance and rhythm, readers have the tools needed for responding to the aural signifiers of a poem. In broad terms, that response can be manifested in two basic ways. In the first place, the reader can identify and explain the ways that aural signifiers construct or enhance meaning; for example, the ways certain words contribute to a tone of harshness or sublimity or joviality. This description of the sounds can open up many interesting responses to the poem as a signifying system. In the second place, the reader can interpret the aural signifiers in a vocal performance of the poem. By reading the poem out loud, readers demonstrate their interpretive responses to the poem by the ways they perform the poem.

In some ways at least, the effort to explain the effects of aural signifiers in a poem is akin to explaining why my son sighs when he sees a rainbow or is similar to attempts to spell out the three hundred and forty-one steps of a backward dive in pike position with a double somersault and a half-twist. Ronald Wallace admits, "I tell my students that certain sounds are more appropriate for expressing certain feelings than others. The advice is vague and intuitive, and it is hard to be more precise." (Wallace, 1981, 564) Perhaps by conventional agreement, we have determined that certain sounds are melodious and soothing while others are harsh, sibilant, and abrupt.

On the other hand, even though I caution readers about placing too much confidence in their ability to explain the effects of aural signifiers, I also contend that poetry is a construction of language, the manipulation of the connotation and the sounds and the rhythm of words. Aural signifiers of poetry *can* be meticulously identified, catalogued, and described. But I am not sure that there is adequate significance (at least for most readers) in that approach. Wallace's explanation of the sounds in a poem belongs in a linguistics textbook: "the crisp, precise vowels and consonants shift to muffled labials which move to abrupt fricatives and sibilants and culminate in the violent b's." (567) In the high school classroom, responses to aural signifiers can be creatively and purposefully expressed in oral interpretations, instead of in prosaic explanations of the effects of the signifiers.

My advice then to teachers is to invite students to read poems out loud, and in doing so to encourage students to use the same kind of expressiveness they use when discussing yesterday's basketball game or the latest musical sensation or the virtues of a Big Mac. There is no special way to speak a poem. Students should not be taught a method of vocalizing poetry. Each performance of a poem will be unique because each performer is unique. When my students first heard a recording of Robert Frost reading his poetry in a slow, sonorous way, they laughed. They expected him to read like the movie star Christopher Plummer whom they had heard the week before. My students were not prepared for the range of possibilities in reading a poem. Over the years, I have heard several fine writers read their poetry in person: Stephen Spender, Margaret Atwood, Robert Gibbs, Robert Hawkes, Alden Nowlan, Al Pittman, John Steffler, Earle Birney, Roo Borson, Daphne Marlatt, Milton Acorn, Martha Hillhouse. They did not adopt standardized poetry-reading voices, and they did not all sound like trained actors. Some sounded conversational and expressive, like storytellers who wanted to share, others sounded intimate and confessional, and some intoned their verse as if they were Old Testament prophets. Each poet made use of the resources of speech in his or her own way.

The components of speech include stress, pitch, pace, pauses, tone, accent, and volume. All of these components contribute to the rhythm. In order to explore the operation of these components, have your students experiment by pronouncing the words "I love you" in as many different ways as they can. They will discover that they can place the primary stress on "I" or "love" or "you"; that they can speak in a high pitch or a low pitch, or somewhere in between; that they can speak the words quickly or slowly; that they can use short or long pauses after "I" or "love" or "you"; that they will speak the words differently, depending upon whom they imagine as the audience (their mother, their best friend, or their pet goldfish); that they can speak with an accent; that they can whisper or scream the words. The human voice is an instrument of astonishing variability capable of broadly divergent effects. Unfortunately, most people use their voices in limited ways only. Most of us are embarrassed by our voices, afraid to perform publicly, eager to imitate the standardized speech of our environment. But Edwin Webb's perceptive observation that "speech is personality in action" (Webb, 1985, 64) reminds us how integrally related are personality and language, and how significant growth in language use is for growth in personality.

Nowhere is the expression "performs a text" more apposite than in the oral reading of a poem. Oral reading is like a speech in drama or a rendition of a musical score. Readers are guided by the text, but they interpret the text as well. They vocalize their unique responses to the text. Comparisons are made between Sir Laurence Olivier's Hamlet and Mel Gibson's Hamlet. Olivier and Gibson are honoured for their unique performances, for their interpretive actualizations of words on a page. Readers need to be encouraged to perceive themselves as performers of poems. Perhaps they will need to be sent (sometimes with tape recorders) to the playground, parking lot, washroom, basement, roof, vice-principal's office, the beach in order to have a quiet place for speaking and rehearsing poems. Eventually the reader's continued interaction with the poem can lead to a public performance (individually or as part of a group) which demonstrates a unique response to the poem.

I am recommending, then, repeated oral readings of a poem culminating in a vocal performance which comprises an understanding of and response to the poem. When students seek to determine the performative voice they will use to read a poem, they should first construct a story for the poem by considering the questions, Who? Where? What? When? Why? Then, guided by considerations of diction, syntax, punctuation, lineation, line-breaks, stanzaic structure, and lay-out, they can ask questions about the many ways they might perform the poem. What is the tone they want to adopt for reading the poem? Will they read it slowly and quietly? Will they read it loudly and harshly? Will they use a range of moods in between these two extremes?

An Illustration of Responding to the Sounds of a Poem
Consider the following poem:

The Addict
by Anne Sexton

Sleepmonger,
deathmonger,
with capsules in my palms each night,
eight at a time from sweet pharmaceutical bottles
I make arrangements for a pint-sized journey.
I'm the queen of this condition.
I'm an expert on making the trip
and now they say I'm an addict.
Now they ask why.
Why!

Don't they know
that I promised to die!
I'm keeping in practice.
I'm merely staying in shape.
The pills are a mother, but better,
every color and as good as sour balls.
I'm on a diet from death.

Yes, I admit
it has gotten to be a bit of a habit–
blows eight at a time, socked in the eye,
hauled away by the pink, the orange,
the green and the white goodnights.
I'm becoming something of a chemical
mixture.
That's it!

My supply
of tablets

has got to last for years and years.
I like them more than I like me.
Stubborn as hell, they won't let go.
It's a kind of marriage.
It's a kind of war
where I plant bombs inside
of myself.

Yes
I try
to kill myself in small amounts,
an innocuous occupation.
Actually I'm hung up on it.
But remember I don't make too much noise.
And frankly no one has to lug me out
and I don't stand there in my winding sheet.
I'm a little buttercup in my yellow nightie
eating my eight loaves in a row
and in a certain order as in
the laying on of hands
or the black sacrament.

It's a ceremony
but like any other sport
it's full of rules.
It's like a musical tennis match where
my mouth keeps catching the ball.
Then I lie on my altar
elevated by the eight chemical kisses.

What a lay me down this is
with two pink, two orange,
two green, two white goodnights.
Fee-fi-fo-fum—
Now I'm borrowed.
Now, I'm numb.

"The Addict" capitalizes on the aural significance of language: the rhyme of "Sleepmonger,/deathmonger"; the euphony of "sweet pharmaceutical bottles"; the repetition of words "they ask why./Why!"; the assonance of "I promised to die"; the cacophony of "good as sour balls"; the alliteration of "diet from death." As part of my responsive reading of the poem, I recorded a long list of aural signifiers. I was not surprised that the list was lengthy because in my initial readings of the poem, I was immediately impressed by the role of consonance and rhythm. A reading could devote attention to examining the various aural signifiers and suggesting explanations for their semantic effects. For example, a reader could suggest that the repetition of "why" at the end of lines 9 and 10 and the rhyme with "die" in line 12 produce the shrill cry of hysteria. Or that an internal rhyme like "the pills are a mother, but better" highlights the speaker's brazenly nonchalant attitude towards addiction. Or that the assonance of "pint-sized journey" and the alliteration of "merely staying in shape" reinforce the sense of a lack of balance and reason in the speaker's posture. Or that the frequent repetition of "I" echoes the speaker's self-absorption. But I recommend that instead of explaining or interpreting the aural effects, readers can learn how they work by performing them.

Readers can examine the poem by rehearsing several oral readings which lead to vocal performances that represent different readers' responses to the poem. Having established a narrative frame for "The Addict," and guided by vocabulary, sentence structure, punctuation, lineation, line breaks, stanzaic structure, and lay-out, readers can ask questions about the different ways they might perform the text. They can ask questions about the pitch, pace, pauses, tone, stress, accent, and volume they might use in vocalizing "The Addict." How, for example, am I going to speak the first two lines: "Sleepmonger,/deathmonger"? "Monger" like "bong, bong" resonates in the air with a drum-like summons that cannot be ignored. Also, the sound of the words seems almost claustrophobic and connotes the sound of "monster." It is unlikely that students would speak the words in a high pitch unless they wanted to parody the lines. The repetition of sound draws and focusses attention on the juxtaposition of sleep and death, creating a surreal atmosphere.

Have your students consider other aural minutiae of the poem. Most of the first stanza could be read in a slow, teasing voice with a hint of menace. Have them consider how the tone in the last two lines changes. The lines are shorter than the six lines which precede them and recall the short lines at the beginning of the stanza. But the tone of the last two lines is significantly different from the tone of the first two lines. Instead of the resonating, drum-like sound of "Sleepmonger,/deathmonger," the stanza ends with the shrill rapid-fire repetition of "why./Why!"

The textual evidence on which students will base their interpretive readings of the first stanza is not definitive. A poem provides ample latitude for variable readings, so students need to ask questions about the enunciating voice in the poem. It seems unbalanced, seductive, and shrill, bold and crazed, alternating between reason and madness. Does the voice indicate a poseur whose speech reveals meaning by apparently concealing meaning? Is the tone of brazen nonchalance an authentic attitude of resentment or a mask designed to alleviate frustration and fear? Is the voice sarcastic, ironic, playful, satirical, bitter, non-conformist, vulgar? Is the voice pervaded by resignation, confusion, deep-rooted pain, pretence, loneliness? Does the voice betray hints of all these attitudes?

These are questions students need to confront in order to expand and strengthen their understanding of the poem. As students face these questions, they will read the poem in different ways with different moods, emphases, pitches, paces. Their repeated readings will contribute to their growing understanding of the poem. In a sense, the oral performer becomes the "I" of the poem, and, therefore, must be able to understand and identify with the "I."

I have concentrated on Anne Sexton's "The Addict" because it makes use of many aural signifiers and makes demands on the oral performer. Even though many poems make fewer demands on the oral performer than "The Addict" does, the procedure for vocalizing poems is essentially the same. The reader needs to read the poem over and over until its aural signifiers are realized in the comprehension of the poem, until the aural signifiers help heighten and order and reflect and structure the meaning-making experience which is fundamental to reading. As readers interact with the text, they impress their own personalities and experiences and emotions and responses on it.

Eventually students can share their responses to the poem in an oral performance. Tom Schmidt suggests that "the poem is not finished until it is performed," (Schmidt, 1981, 134) but I argue that a poem is never finished; it always remains open to more performances. A vocal reading of a poem will not be the definitive reading of the poem. Each reader will present a unique responsive transaction with the sounds of the poem.

Responding to a Poem that Resists Reading

In this section, as well as in the final sections of the book, I present strategies for responding to poetry that acknowledge readily the complexity of poetry as well as the frustration many readers experience when they read poetry. At the beginning of the book, I spelled out the overarching design of the book by explaining that the reader-response orientation is the general perspective which grounds all of the strategies. I also suggested that semiotics, deconstruction, and cultural criticism are useful orientations for informing the reader-response orientation. The book began with strategies that are fun and inviting. The following strategies will be fun and inviting, too, but they will also be demanding since they involve grappling with resistant texts.

Teachers and students alike need to remember the following points when tackling the texts of difficult poems.

(1)   Anything in a poem can signify—words, phrases, clauses, sentences (diction and syntax), the poem's line breaks and stanzaic structure, its punctuation and capitalization, the title, shape, margins, spaces, typescript, and spelling, and its layout on the page. Therefore, the basic questions teachers and students need to ask themselves in regard to each of these elements of a poem are, "What can this mean?" and "What does this do?"

(2)   The working tools for reading poetry can be developed during the reading process. Instead of being drilled in a long list of terminology, students can acquire a working knowledge of rhetorical figures as they confront poems and raise questions. It might be objected that if students don't know what an apostrophe is, they will not recognize the rhetorical figure when they meet it in a poem. However, if students are reading with the operational notion that everything signifies, then they will likely recognize the special use of language that is labelled "apostrophe." They

might not have in their repertoire the convenient term to call it "an address to an imaginary or absent person or thing," (Bremner, 1984, 54) but they can still recognize the figure, and, more importantly, incorporate the figure into their meaning-making activity. Meanwhile, the teacher can take the opportunity to share a definition of apostrophe with the class.

(3) Reading a poem employs the same operations used in reading prose. In both cases, we read from left to right; that is, we read teleologically, constantly constructing, augmenting, and revising our meaning-making as we proceed through the text. We define words and interpret punctuation according to conventions and we interact subjectively with the text so that our personalities, experiences, and knowledge are integrally involved in the production of understanding. For all the helter-skelter activity involved in reading, it is ultimately a pattern-making procedure intent on constructing order. Poetry seems generically more obscure than prose because the tradition of prose writing valorizes prose that is clear and plainly comprehensible whereas poetry is less obviously transparent. To read poetry the reader must be willing to linger with the text. Recalling Roland Barthes' suggestion that much of our reading is done in the gaps when we lift up our heads from the text and reflect and postulate and organize, I think that more reading is typically done in the gaps while reading poetry than while reading prose. In other words, poetry slows readers down. As a teacher I frequently share my readings with my students in order to show them the slow and detailed manner in which I interact with poems.

To begin practising the preceding principles the following poem is a useful starting place because it is brief and elliptical:

Dietrich Bonhoffer at the Gallows
by Raymond Souster

The noose
fitting snugly like a parson's collar.

Before looking at the words in Souster's poem, I want to emphasize a significant and frequently overlooked aspect of language. It is not unusual to stress that poetry frequently employs figurative language, with the implication that only some language is figurative (perhaps that which is ornate and sensual), but all language is figurative in that it contains a figure, a sign that points to something else. When combined in a particular configuration, the letters "b," "a," "l," "l" signify a round object. There is no inherent reason why this specific organization of the letters must signify a round object, but conventional agreement has established this connection. And not only does "ball" signify a round object, but it can signify a plethora of round objects—big balls and little balls, red balls and blue balls, deflated and inflated balls, cannon balls and meatballs, ball-bearings and ball-cocks, footballs and balls of the feet, eyeballs and spitballs. And as if that isn't already sufficiently complicated, "ball" also refers to a dance, a good time, or a sexual encounter. While a single word can have many possible significations, its use in a particular context and its connections with other words limit the possible meanings a reader will generate. Close attention to the eight words of Souster's poem can lead students to understand the many ways in which words can signify while teaching them the necessity of limiting the connotations they assign to particular words by reading them in the context of their neighbours.

Reading "Dietrich Bonhoffer at the Gallows," students need to consider the connotations of "noose," "fitting snugly," and "parson's collar." A noose is the loop in a hangman's rope, a means of execution, even painful death, a symbol of capital punishment, and the right and responsibility of the state to exact justice. "Fitting snugly" has connotations of comfort and warmth, but it can also suggest tightness and restriction. A parson's collar is a symbol, not only of a minister's vocation, but of the Christian church and almost two thousand years of church history and Christian belief and practice.

By relating these words in a simile, Souster expands their connotations. The comparison between the noose and the parson's collar will be enigmatic for some readers. Some might conjecture that since ministers always preside at executions, the connection between "noose" and "parson's collar" is not so strange. Nevertheless, the description of "the noose/fitting snugly like a parson's collar" is fraught with ambiguity. It is hard to imagine that the noose fits comfortably unless the person to be hanged welcomes his execution. Moreover, in what ways does a parson's collar "fit snugly"? It is a public sign of dedication to the Christian belief-system and commitment to a life modelled after Jesus Christ. The collar signifies both the security and the challenge of faith so it, too, is ambiguous. Perhaps the poem could be interpreted as a minister's feeling of discomfort as he presides over the execution of a man; his collar feels tight. Or maybe he is struck by the oddity of the noose looking like his collar. The two are so dissimilar and yet. . . .

The most significant words in the poem are probably in the title. Who is Dietrich Bonhoffer? Is he being hanged? Is he observing the hanging? Most young readers will not know that Dietrich Bonhoffer was a prestigious German theologian and pastor who actively opposed Hitler and was hanged in 1945. But the allusion to Bonhoffer echoes with ramifications far beyond the historical facts of his life. The name "Dietrich Bonhoffer" no longer refers only to a theologian and pastor who conspired to assassinate Hitler and was killed for his efforts. The name "Dietrich Bonhoffer" has become a sign for militant Christianity, martyrdom, and total commitment to a cause.

Knowing this information about Dietrich Bonhoffer, the reader is directed to identify the comparison between the noose and the collar. While in prison awaiting his execution Bonhoffer wrote, "Death is the supreme festival on the road to freedom," (Bonhoffer, 1967, 206) and "The Church is the Church only when it exists for others." (211) For all of their apparent dissimilarity, then, "the noose" and "a parson's collar" have much in common. Bonhoffer is a symbol for the attitude that Christianity is a way of life devoted to ignominy, service, confrontation with the world, and sacrifice.

In spite of its brevity (and partly because of its brevity), Souster's poem courts the active engagement of the reader in making meaning. Even in a poem as brief as "Dietrich Bonhoffer at the Gallows," it is useful to consider the lineation. Souster could have written the poem as one line, but by putting "the noose" (just two syllables) on a line by itself, the words are isolated, framed, and highlighted. With the line break there is a pause, and the reader's attention is focused both spatially and temporally on this richly suggestive word. Then the starkness of the first line is complemented by the much longer second line with its slower pace and words of typically positive connotation.

A semiotic reading of the following poem again illustrates how a poem is a network of signs that relate to one another in order to create meaningful effects:

The Fist
by Derek Walcott

The fist clenched round my heart
loosens a little, and I gasp
brightness; but it tightens
again. When have I ever not loved
the pain of love? But this has moved

past love to mania. This has the strong
clench of the madman, this is
gripping the ledge of unreason, before
plunging howling into the abyss.

Hold hard then, heart. This way at least you live.

In a purely subjective response, we might relate the poem's treatment of love to our own experiences of and notions about love. For example, I might sigh or groan, and confess that Walcott's perception is acute and accurate. But my pleasure in the text is enhanced as I explore the effects of the poem's construction semiotically. Teachers can begin with a simple question, What are the effects of the lineation? In this poem the syntax is straightforward; the sentences could be written as prose. So what do the line breaks do? By reading each line with a pause signalled by the line break, I know a keen edge of suspense. What is coming next? And yet with no punctuation at the end of the line (except at the end of stanza two), the pause is not reinforced, and I am compelled forward, glad to continue.

I realize that this kind of explanation is probably not going to enthuse Ralph whose attention is focussed on the clock and the bells. The effect I want to describe is rather obscure, but it is integral to all reading and especially heightened in the reading of poetry. Readers are constantly looking back and forward. As they traverse the text they are constantly establishing expectations of what is going to come on the basis of what they have read, and then modifying those expectations and positing more. And through this reading process there is an unfolding semantic movement, a sense of ebb and flow. In "The Fist," for example, the fourth line ends with "When have I ever not loved," and the expectation is that the next line will continue with "you" or some reference to a person, so the reader may be surprised by the predicate object, "the pain of love." Expecting a conventional object, the reader may be impressed by a conclusion which is an oxymoron. Instead of claiming love for a person, the speaker confesses love for "the pain of love."

In my reading, then, the division into lines produces significant semantic effects by encouraging and circumventing expectations. But the line divisions are also mimetic: they imitate on the page the action signified by the words. For example, stanza one ends with "But this has moved," and there is then not only the space at the end of the line, but also the wide space that indicates the division into stanzas. So the action of movement in line five is mimetically signified in the movement across a gap to another stanza.

After the unfolding movement of syntax and semantics in the first two stanzas, the final stanza is two sentences comprising just one line. Resolve and forthrightness are expressed in the line. Not only is it syntactically separated from the other stanzas, but it is also the longest line in the poem. So it has a jutting appearance, thereby further illustrating its pre-eminence.

There are clearly many other elements of Walcott's poem that could be read, including the metaphors of the fist and the heart, the paradox of life in pain and mania, the apostrophic address to the heart, and the use of declarative, interrogative, and imperative sentences, but concentration on the division of lines and stanzaic structure illustrates that questions about the effects of these elements in a poem contributes to an understanding of the poem. George Bowering asks, "Why stop a line and begin anew unless such break in the flow means something?" (Bowering, 1983, 347) There is no standard answer that can be presented in order to explain all the effects of line divisions or different stanzaic structures used in poems. While there are some conventional patterns—the sonnet, the villanelle, the sestina—most poetry (and especially most contemporary poetry) follows no prescribed pattern. Indeed, poets even experiment with the traditional patterns in creative variations.

Each of the following exercises focuses on semiotic approaches to reading poetry.

ACTIVITY

Select a poem that uses interesting lineation and stanzaic structure. Without showing the original poem to the students, write the poem as a passage of prose, and invite students to construct the poem in lines and stanzas, and then compare their versions of the poem with the original. In providing a rationale for their choices, students will be consciously engaging in the kind of creative processes that the poet engages in, processes which are governed by the semiotic potential of poetic writing.

ACTIVITY

In order to explore the effect of titles on reading poems, share several poems with students, but omit the titles and ask them to supply titles. Then compare with the original titles. How do different titles work as signs to indicate how the poem can be read?

ACTIVITY

Print the following poem in large letters on a sheet of construction paper.

Track
by Tomas Tranströmer

2 a.m.: moonlight. The train has stopped
out in a field. Far off sparks of light from a town,
flickering coldly on the horizon.

As when a man goes so deep into his dream
he will never remember that he was there
when he returns again to his room.

Or when a person goes so deep into a sickness
that his days all become some flickering sparks, a swarm,
feeble and cold on the horizon.

The train is entirely motionless.
2 o'clock: strong moonlight, few stars.

Cut up the sheet of paper into strips with one line on each strip and mix up the pieces. Ask students to arrange the lines in an order that pleases them. Then have them compare their efforts with Tranströmer's poem. What are the semiotic effects of different arrangements of the lines?

ACTIVITY

In small groups students could respond to the following poem with attention to the semantic effects of diction, syntax, lineation, patterns, and organization.

Epilogue
by Denise Levertov

I thought I had found a swan
but it was a migrating snow-goose.

I thought I was linked invisibly to another's life
but I found myself more alone with him than without him.

I thought I had found a fire
but it was the play of light on bright stones.

I thought I was wounded to the core
but I was only bruised.

Every poem invites multiple responses, and students need to be reminded that a poem does not have a single interpretation. The following responses to "Epilogue" illustrate some ways that the teacher might guide students in responding to some aspects of the poem. For anybody who has ever fallen in love and then fallen out of love, the experience described in "Epilogue" is familiar. Its clear pattern has the bare, stark lines of a piece of traditional Shaker furniture. There are four stanzas and each stanza is one sentence organized in two lines. The first line begins with "I thought" and the second line with "but" (the conjunction of contrast). The pattern uses parallelism, and as the Hebrew poets knew, parallelism is an effective way to express an observation, emotion, or idea by accumulative repetition.

The title "Epilogue" indicates a summation at the end of a discourse, and the pattern of the poem impresses with its definitive quality. Each stanza is a separate unit. The "but" is foregrounded in its position at the beginning of a line and the period at the end of the stanza indicates an emphatic pause, the cumulative effect of the pause at the end of a line compounded by the pause indicated by the period. Each stanza is so much like each other stanza that there is the effect of an echo resounding loudly and clearly, with mounting emphasis.

A further contribution of the pattern to the semantic effects is that in stanzas one and three the first lines have active verbs ("had found") and in stanzas two and four the first lines have passive verbs ("was linked," "was wounded") so the speaker has now gotten over the experience completely, in both the active and passive aspects of the experience.

A semiotic reading will pay attention to the relationships between the pairs of words: "swan/snow-goose," "linked/alone," "fire/play of light," and "wounded/bruised," as well as the punctuation, the use of the pronouns "I" and "it," the imagery, and the genre of lyric love poetry.

After reading poems informed by a semiotic understanding of how a poem works as a text, students will be ready to tease out the plural meanings that a poem can have. The theoretical perspective of deconstruction provides useful tools for reading poems with imagination and insight.

CHAPTER 4

Deconstruction

By 1985 I had taught secondary school English for eight years, years that were frequently fraught with frustration and a fulsome sense of futility, years when I often felt that I was surrounded by people, young and old, who knew no joy in word-making and word-weaving. In my early thirties I was eager to revel in a community of wordsmiths. I enrolled in a graduate program in English literature and creative writing. In my first class I was introduced to deconstruction, and even though I left the class confused and nervously evaluating my aptitude for graduate studies, I was elated with the promise of deconstruction for transforming the experiences of readers. In fact, I was so enamoured with deconstruction that I completed the master's degree followed by a second master's followed by a doctorate, all significantly informed by deconstruction. Armed with three graduate degrees, I returned to secondary school English teaching, and I learned that even though deconstruction is no carpetbag of tools and potions for alleviating the ills frequently experienced in English education classes, deconstruction does offer new ways of conceiving and framing the underlying assumptions and goals and activities that characterize many English education classes.

Deconstruction is rooted in the philosophical perspective that the world is constructed and disclosed in language. Using a rigorously critical approach, deconstruction demonstrates that language carries multiple meanings. As an approach to composing and responding to texts, deconstruction goes beyond obvious and superficial understandings, and seeks to reveal how language can be interpreted in many different ways and how language works rhetorically to create meanings.

Above all, deconstruction celebrates interrogation, play, and imaginative meaning-making. Why are schools so often places without joy, laughter, fun? Years ago I saw a comic strip featuring two mice called Eek and Meek. In one frame they are walking side by side. Then Eek jumps into the air and clicks his heels. Meek is affronted: "Knock it off. Life is serious." The fourth frame shows Eek and Meek once again walking side by side, subdued, composed, appropriately engaged in the contemplation of the serious life. How often do schools transmit the resounding cry, "Life is serious"? There is little time for fun, at least in schools. Schools are constituted and maintained with an air of grave decorum where children are prepared (manufactured, produced, moulded) for the serious life. Students are discouraged from jumping into the air and clicking their heels, and it is no wonder that by graduation many young people have forgotten they ever could.

The chagrin and resentment that deconstruction has engendered in many academic and professional circles is a clear sign of the reluctance of some people to acknowledge an approach to language that posits "game" and "play" and "fun" as inherent features of language. Proponents of deconstruction have been accused of nefarious activities ranging from purposeful obscurity to undermining the humanist tradition. They have been called subversive trouble-makers and nihilistic jokesters.

Without question, deconstruction undermines long-held assumptions about language and language use. It is also true that those writers who are enamoured with deconstruction are often obscure. Their writing can be labyrinthine. Moreover, because deconstructionists are pre-eminent questioners (often asking more questions than providing answers), they upset people who like to believe there are more answers than questions. Nevertheless, my own reaction to deconstruction is instructive because it has been primarily constructive. Deconstruction motivates me to read with imagination, with a sense of fun, with an awareness of play in language. Near vending machines there is often a machine which is designed to provide coins when paper currency is inserted. The instructions include: DO NOT FOLD BILL/INSERT BILL FACE UP INTO BILL ACCEPTOR. Trained as most readers are to seek out the plain, obvious meaning, most people will interpret the sign to mean that there is a specific procedure to be followed in inserting a five-dollar bill into the machine if a person wants coins. But whenever I read those instructions, I think about my friend Bill, and about trying to squeeze his two hundred pounds into the bill acceptor.

Of course, it can be protested that common sense tells the reader what the sign "really" means, but common sense is the protective armour of that view that contends, "Life is serious." Common sense is the product of convention, not an external or absolute verity. And, anyway, is it not more fun to read the sign in new ways? T.S. Eliot reminds us in "Burnt Norton" that "Words strain/Crack and sometimes break, under the burden,/Under the tension, slip, slide, perish,/Decay with imprecision, will not stay in place." (Eliot, 1971, 19) It is a facile assumption that words are vehicles for communicating clear, evident meanings. Words are often more seductive than productive, always promising precision and delivering delusion, never quite saying what you thought you said or heard, what you meant or thought was meant.

Deconstruction has been castigated for its fundamental assumption that language is untameable for both the reader and the writer. It is argued that deconstruction precludes the possibility of communication and that it fails to pay adequate attention to the common experience of people who do, in fact, manage to understand one another. Deconstruction has been vilified for claiming that language can never mean anything, that meaning cannot be arrived at because the reader can always propose another different interpretation. But what deconstruction really objects to is interpretive closure. There can be no univocal, authoritative reading of a text. There is always something more. Deconstruction encourages a multiplicity of responses. It promotes playing with texts. It celebrates the wildness of language.

What is especially attractive about deconstruction for the secondary school classroom is that young readers do not have to be intimidated by the self-conscious fear that their responses to a text are wrong. There are no right and wrong answers. Deconstruction encourages a plurality of responses. There is no hidden meaning that must be revealed. The text is a site where the reader's imagination and experience and understanding and emotions come into play in unique and imaginative performances. The goal of deconstruction is to open up the text, which becomes not a puzzle to be laboriously pieced together, but a stage on which to perform.

Instead of reading for a harmonious and totalizing comprehension of a text, deconstruction recommends an approach to reading that seeks to avoid resolution by acknowledging the slipping and sliding indeterminacy of language use. Instead of ascertaining the apparently obvious meaning of a text, the reader is encouraged to pay attention to elements in the text that contradict one another or do not cohere or are obscure. In a deconstructive spirit, students can sabotage conventions, court flagrant silliness, interrogate ruthlessly, scoff at claims of truth, wallow in meaning-making (not the solved meaning), and have fun. They can produce alternative (even conflicting) readings of a text, and revel in the openness of a text that invites different responses.

This is not to say that a deconstructive approach lacks discipline. On the contrary. Deconstructive reading is self-conscious reading; nothing is taken for granted. Readers are motivated and influenced in their reading by their personalities, values, experiences, education, and command of conventional strategies for reading. Their practices of reading arc informed by both personal and communal matrices of expectations and assumptions. By being aware of these personal and communal matrices, readers can adopt different perspectives in relation to the text as a site for the production of multiple meanings.

Jacques Derrida has argued convincingly that the world is constructed and disclosed in language use, and that close attention needs to be given especially to the ways that writing produces and constrains meaning-making. Informed by Derrida, Roland Barthes claims that reading is an active process of engagement between readers and texts, while Paul de Man exposes the ways that texts are always riddled with gaps and contradictions. And Barbara Johnson explores the connections between texts and other texts, while Shoshana Felman investigates how subject identities and perspectives are shaped by reading and writing. It is not easy, and perhaps not feasible, to define deconstruction. Christopher Norris cautions: "To present 'deconstruction' as if it were a method, a system or a settled body of ideas would be to falsify its nature and lay oneself open to charges of reductive misunderstanding." (Norris, 1982, 1) Nevertheless, in spite of Norris's caution, I suggest the following definition: deconstruction is a practice of reading which claims that meaning is a textual construction. Therefore, a text is not a window that a reader can look through in order to see the author's intention or some essential and universal truth, nor is the text a mirror that reflects a colourful image of the reader's experience or wisdom. Instead, deconstruction is reading in order to make meaning from a text by focussing attention on the rhetoric of the text and how a text is connected to other texts as well as the historical, cultural, social, and political contexts in which texts are written, read, published, reviewed, rewarded, and distributed.

In the past two decades no approach to reading has had more impact than deconstruction on literary criticism and the teaching of literature. Deconstruction is at the heart of the reading approaches presented in this book because deconstruction honours readers and their responses without making readers the sole source of meaning-making. Moreover, deconstruction builds on the spirit of semiotics with its focus on a text as a system of signs. Finally, deconstruction looks to the wide-ranging cultural criticism approaches of Marxism, historicism, feminism, postcolonialism, and issues of race (discussed in chapter five) where the focus is on interrogating the taken-for-granted assumptions that guide the ways texts are written and read in different ideological contexts. In my secondary school classes, I introduced deconstructive approaches to reading poetry, and I continue to share these approaches with my current students in English education courses, because reading poetry is more productive and more fun when readers understand that they are engaging in the deconstruction of a constructed text in order to help reconstruct it.

In this section I illustrate five different ways for reading poetry informed by deconstruction: by considering self-referential aspects of the poem; by reading the poem from different perspectives; by considering the binary oppositions the poem establishes; by considering the different readings made possible through its use of figurative and literal language; and by considering in what ways the poem is intertextual. Following a discussion of these five approaches illustrated by readings of several poems, I provide several exercises by which your students could use all of these approaches to respond to one poem.

Self-Referentiality

In one of my favourite Norman Rockwell illustrations, Norman Rockwell is drawing an illustration of Norman Rockwell while watching Norman Rockwell drawing in a mirror. This illustration reminds me how intricate and complex are the dynamics of perspective and perception in literature. To whom does the "I" in a poem refer, for example? Does the "I" refer to the author, or the speaker, or the reader? Are authors responsible for all responses to their texts? Do authors control the dynamics at work in their texts? What is the relationship between the world of the text and the empirical world? A deconstructive approach to reading a poem precludes simplistic identifications between the world of the poem and the world of the reader and the world of the poet. Instead the reader acknowledges the textual construction or rhetoric of the poem, the ways that various strategies and tropes and conventions work together to create particular effects. Paying attention to the self-referentiality of a poem is a way of not forgetting that the poem is a textual construct. In the following poem "To Julia de Burgos" by Julia de Burgos, self-referentiality is foregrounded. "To Julia de Burgos" examines the relationship between the empirical world and the world of the poem, between the poet as a person in society and the poet as a voice in her poetry, between the "I" in the poem and the "I" of the poet. Many poems are not as blatantly self-referential as "To Julia de Burgos," but deconstructive reading seeks out the ways that all texts are constructed and available for deconstructing and reconstructing.

To Julia de Burgos
by Julia de Burgos

The people are saying that I am your enemy,
    That in poetry I give you to the world.

    They lie, Julia de Burgos. They lie, Julia de Burgos.
The voice that rises in my verses is not your voice: it
    is my voice;
For you are the clothing and I am the essence;
Between us lies the deepest abyss.

You are the bloodless doll of social lies
And I the virile spark of human truth;

You are the honey of courtly hypocrisy; not I–
I bare my heart in all my poems.

You, like your world, are selfish; not I–
I gamble everything to be what I am.

You are only the serious lady. Señora. Doña Julia.
Not I. I am life. I am strength. I am woman.

You belong to your husband, your master. Not I:
I belong to nobody or to all, for to all, to all
I give myself in my pure feelings and thoughts.

You curl your hair and paint your face. Not I:
I am curled by the wind, painted by the sun.

You are the lady of the house, resigned, submissive,
Tied to the bigotry of men. Not I:
I an Rocinante, bolting free, wildly
Snuffling the horizons of the justice of God.

The Puerto Rican poet named Julia de Burgos (known to her family and friends and readers as Julia de Burgos) has written a poem addressed to Julia de Burgos in which the speaker denies that Julia de Burgos is responsible for or even involved in the poetry which bears her name as its author. Instead the enunciating voice declares to Julia de Burgos that "The voice that rises in my verses is not your voice: it is my voice." My first question to the poem, then, is, Would the real Julia de Burgos please stand up? There is the Julia de Burgos who lived from 1914 to 1953, was raised in rural Puerto Rico, participated in the labour union movement, suffered from alcoholism, and gained recognition as an important writer only after her death. At least the name of this Julia de Burgos has been ascribed as the author of the poem. There is also the Julia de Burgos addressed in the title and described in the poem as "the bloodless doll of social lies," "the honey of courtly hypocrisy," and "the lady of the house, resigned, submissive." Then there is the unnamed speaker of the poem, a poet who claims that between her and Julia de Burgos "lies the deepest abyss," even though they are still related, at least as opposites: "For you are the clothing and I am the essence."

The poem is like a room of mirrors in which Julia de Burgos is reflected from many different angles, and it is impossible to discern the real Julia de Burgos from her images. The poem is illusory: the speaker emphatically contends that she is no enemy of Julia de Burgos: "The people are saying that I am your enemy,/That in poetry I give you to the world./They lie, Julia de Burgos. They lie, Julia de Burgos." But the poem is a strong polemic castigating Julia de Burgos and revealing her to the world as false, facile, fatuous, fixed. If the speaker's claim that she is not an enemy and that others are liars is a specious claim, then perhaps her other claims are also unreliable, including her claim to be "the virile spark of human truth." For all her insistence that she is "life," "strength," "woman," and that she gives herself in her "pure feelings and thoughts," she seems remarkably self-righteous, bigoted, blind. And yet, thereby, the speaker has unwittingly fulfilled her assertion: "I bare my heart in all my poems." The real Julia de Burgos refuses to step out of the room of mirrors and in the multiplicity of images manifests her identity as plural and undecidable. This poem about poets and poetry, voices and words, lies and truth, is like a room of mirrors casting contradictory reflections and refusing a single focal point from which understanding can be organized and ordered. "To Julia de Burgos" reminds readers that there is no easy passage to the author's intention. The deconstructive emphasis on self-referentiality in a poem resists traditional reading practices of seeking in the poem an expression of authorial intention and autobiographical connection. Readers have learned to equate the narrator's voice in a poem with the voice of the historical person who is called the poet. But deconstruction reminds readers that this practice of identification between the narrator's voice and the poet is a convention of reading. Like all conventions, it is constructed through practice and consensus, and available for deconstruction.

Reading from Different Perspectives

Like reader-response approaches which invite multiple readings by different readers with different experiences, deconstruction promotes multiple ways of reading a poem, especially by inviting readers to interrogate their own responses to the poem as a text. For example, deconstruction reminds the reader to ask questions about the perspectives from which the poem can be read. The reader is encouraged to read from different perspectives, and to acknowledge the ways that the poetic text invites, not closure, but a dissemination of plural readings. For example, when I read a poem, I sometimes focus attention on how a male reader might respond and how a female reader might respond. I consider the reliability of the narrator in the poem. I question my responses. Students need to consider what perspectives the poem invites them to occupy or what perspectives are available for them as readers. The following poem offers an enticing invitation to read from different perspectives.

This Is a Photograph of Me
by Margaret Atwood

It was taken some time ago.
At first it seems to be
a smeared
print: blurred lines and grey flecks
blended with the paper;

then, as you scan
it, you see in the left-hand corner
a thing that is like a branch: part of a tree
(balsam or spruce) emerging
and, to the right, halfway up
what ought to be a gentle
slope, a small frame house.

In the background there is a lake,
and beyond that, some low hills.

(The photograph was taken
the day after I drowned.

I am in the lake, in the center
of the picture, just under the surface.

It is difficult to say where
precisely, or to say
how large or small I am:
the effect of water
on light is a distortion

but if you look long enough,
eventually
you will be able to see me.)

    "This is a Photograph of Me" raises some perplexing questions about the perspective from which the reader needs to approach the poem. The "I" invites a "you" to look at a photograph. The "I" (or the voice or speaker) claims to be dead. The photograph is hardly a photograph at all—it is smeared, blurred, indistinct. Even though the voice of the poem is conversational, not unlike a sister sharing pictures of a recent vacation at the lakeside, her conversational, matter-of-fact tone only foregrounds the strangeness of the enunciative situation. I refer to the speaker as female because the poet is female, but, of course, that is an arbitrary decision.

    How can students be encouraged to respond to the mysterious nature of the poem? There are a number of distinct perspectives from which the student can be encouraged to read. You might suggest that, since the speaker has drowned, in the poem she is nothing more than a ghost or spirit. In the real world we may have doubts about the existence of ghosts, but in a fictional world where anything can happen we may be more than willing to accept the activity of a ghost. Or students might assume that the speaker is mad and unbalanced, deranged with delusions of her own death—convinced she is dead and struggling to convince others. Or perhaps she is an inveterate wit, the life of the party, a jokester who has seen every Steve Martin movie. In that case, the comedy might be black humour or whimsy or satire. Or maybe she's drunk and a whining bore who likes to pretend she's dead in order to secure sympathy. Or perhaps the poem can be used as an allegory of the way the speaker feels, a metaphorical expression of her sense of being unnoticed, insignificant, worthless. Any one of these positions for reading the poem can lead to fruitful discussion. But examining all of the positions together can lead to a bountiful harvest of inquiry.

By pursuing the implications of dissimilar, and even conflicting, perspectives for reading the poem, teachers can demonstrate the polyvalence of the text to their students, the multiplicitous unfolding of the signifiers. Teachers should also be careful to indicate how actively involved they are, and their students should be, as readers in constructing the significance of the text. While I explore the different perspectives, I most readily adopt the stance that the speaker is sharing intimately with me her sense of being invisible. Every reader becomes the "you" and as the poem is read and reread may even become the "I." The process by which the reader is drawn into the poem is gradual and circuitous, but convincing. The more the reader looks and looks at the photograph (the photograph that is indistinct, the photograph that isn't really a photograph at all since it is constructed in the words of the poem only, the photograph that is described in increasingly dubious ways like "a thing that is like a branch", "what ought to be a gentle/slope", "It is difficult to say where/precisely", and "the effect of water/on light is a distortion"), the more the reader sees the speaker. Even though the speaker claims to be a drowned body somewhere under the centre of a lake in the background of a blurred picture further distorted by the effect of water on light, I still see her. As she promises, "if you look long enough,/eventually/you will be able to see me." I look and look, and begin to see her not in the photograph (which remains graphically indistinct), but in her desire to be seen. Teachers might ask their students why she is so concerned about being seen. Does she look indistinct because so few people see her? Does she need to be seen in order to "be"?

In a sense the reader is played with in the poem. The speaker conjures a picture out of nothing and the reader sees the picture vividly as a picture of the human urge to self-expression coupled with the incapacity to express the self, the unstinting desire to reveal oneself fulfilled only as others reveal that self. And always that self remains only dimly perceived, a blurred and distorted picture that demands interpretation and involvement.

When teachers invite secondary students to respond to Margaret Atwood's poem, "This Is a Photograph of Me," they may find that their students are initially confused and reluctant to discuss the poem because they cannot make sense of it. They cannot reduce the poem to a clear statement of its paraphraseable content. But when teachers explain that students do not need to find a meaning, but can, instead, generate multiple meanings, the discussion typically becomes enthusiastic.

Binary Oppositions

Deconstruction pays close attention to binary oppositions such as light/dark, good/evil, love/hate, strength/weakness. Such binary oppositions involve a value-laden hierarchy with one element given priority over the other. Deconstructive reading contests this order of priority. By calling into question the typical attitude towards the hierarchical ordering of the elements in a binary opposition, readers can enjoy the production of fresh insights. The poignant significance of the following brief poem is disclosed as the reader ruminates on the binary opposition between reason and anti-reason.

A Wonder
by Sakutaro Hagiwara

Reason cannot even refute anti-reason.

"A Wonder" sets up a binary opposition. The relation between an idea and its opposite is a relation of distance and tension. The customary attitude to a binary opposition is to valorize one idea over the other. Hence, love is privileged over hate and gentleness over violence. But if readers examine a binary opposition by calling into question the typical attitude towards the hierarchical ordering of the elements, they can arrive at new understandings. When I began reading "A Wonder," my initial reaction was a nod of recognition—yes, I had often used reason in argument and debate (sound, strong reason, I thought), but I couldn't dislodge those views riddled with anti-reason. The real problem must be all those people who refuse to listen to reason, I concluded. But as I continued reading, I admitted that not only is it true that "reason cannot even refute anti-reason," but it is equally true that "anti-reason cannot even refute reason." Of course, reason cannot refute anti-reason. Reason and anti-reason are opposites. They are separate and in tension. Whatever is regarded as reason (and it might not be reasonable to suggest that there is objective, ultimate reason since reason might be based finally on faith or consensus), its opposite is anti-reason. So, if reason contends that "love is good" or "evil is good," then anti-reason contends that "love is not good" or "evil is not good."

"A Wonder" makes a claim for reason which is unreasonable. The word "even" is significant because it implies the inefficacy of reason. But it is futile to castigate reason for failing to refute what cannot be refuted. Reason and anti-reason are defined and understood in relation to one another.

My response to "A Wonder" illustrates the way that a reader can linger with a poem in order to tease out some of the possible meanings that might be missed or ignored in a reading that takes for granted the way one element is valorized over the other in a binary opposition. Students need to develop an interrogative stance towards all poems. There is a poignant demonstration of this interrogative approach in the film *Malcolm X* when the camera focusses on the dictionary entries that define "black" and "white." One colour is extolled while the other is vilified. *Malcolm X* seeks to open up the possibilities of understanding the words in new ways. Students need to be continually alert to the ways that language is used.

Figurative/Literal Language

Consider the typical approach to figurative language in poetry. Because students are informed that a poem characteristically employs figurative language, they are always searching for symbolism and metaphors. A rose is apparently never a rose when referred to in a poem; it must be a symbol for love or beauty or life. Deconstruction reverses this common approach by suggesting that where a text courts a figurative interpretation, readers could interpret the language literally, and where a text courts a literal reading, readers could interpret the language figuratively. In one of my classes my grade ten students and I read Alfred Lord Tennyson's "The Eagle." When I read the line about the eagle clinging to the crag, Peter leaned forward and fastened his outspread fingers around the head of the student in front of him whose name was appropriately Craig. A conventional reading approach suppresses the play of the language. By questioning and juxtaposing literal and figurative language, the text is opened up for new opportunities of interaction. A deconstructive reading of the following poem pays attention to the figurative and literal language in order to open up the text to plural interpretations.

The Hanging Man
by Sylvia Plath

By the roots of my hair some god got hold of me.
I sizzled in his blue volts like a desert prophet.

The nights snapped out of sight like a lizard's eyelid:
A world of bald white days in a shadeless socket.

A vulturous boredom pinned me in this tree.
If he were I, he would do what I did.

Most readers who encounter "The Hanging Man" by Sylvia Plath are impressed by the unusual figurative language which helps produce a surreal effect. In turn, most readers are willing to enter into a sense of heightened emotion in response to the language. But instead of looking through the figurative language to its effects, instead of reading the poem as a cry of frustration and despair, a deconstructive reading undertakes to examine both "the figural and literal powers of the signifier." (De Man, 1985, 56)

My own effort to explore the literal significance of figurative signifiers and the figurative significance of literal signifiers in "The Hanging Man" includes the following queries and comments. How can anybody get hold of somebody by the roots of her hair? What does getting hold of somebody by the roots of her hair mean? Could a god penetrate the skull and get hold of the brain, which is located near the roots? What kind of god gets hold of people and sizzles them? Is a desert prophet sizzled by blue volts or is a desert prophet like the god's blue volts? Did the speaker look like a desert prophet after sizzling? What does a desert prophet look like? What are blue volts? What does "sizzled" mean?

Of course nights snap out of sight: nights are dark, or at least eyelids are usually closed. But here the speaker indicates that the nights have disappeared. How could there be no nights? Does a lizard have eyelids? I don't think so. Having been held by the roots of her hair and sizzled, it is not surprising that she regards the days as "bald" and "white." A "shadeless socket" could be an electrical socket or an eye socket or a "sock-it-to-me."

Are the "god" and the "vulturous boredom" synonymous? What is "a vulturous boredom"? How can boredom be vulturous? How can boredom pin somebody in a tree? How can a god who sizzles with blue volts be boring? I think about blue suede shoes and blue sizzling volts. How does the speaker know that the vulturous boredom would do what she did? What does she mean by "he would do what I did"? What did she do? The only thing I know she did was write a poem. Would he really have done that? What tree? Was the poem written while in the tree? If she were he, would she do what he did? Who is "the hanging man" in the title? The speaker who was hanged? The god doing the hanging (a god then who is really a man)?

By reading the poem in this deconstructive way I am playing with it. A conventional reading stance towards the poem suppresses the play of the signifiers. By questioning and juxtaposing the figurative and the literal signifiers of the poem, by revealing its undecidability, its gaps, the poem is opened up for new avenues of interaction. John Brenkman observes that "the two sides of reading poetry are a dialectic . . . between floating attention and the moment-to-conclude" (Brenkman, 1985, 185). It is important not to conclude too quickly because a poem always raises more questions than it provides answers. Eventually the poetry class or poetry unit or school year will end, and so there are always those moments when conclusion must be announced, but the conclusion ought to be due to the restraints of time, not the notion that the poem is finished.

Intertextuality

Every text is related to other texts. Intertextuality refers to the ways a text overlaps with other texts, and cites other texts, and assumes a knowledge of other texts. How are readers' responses influenced by their knowledge or lack of knowledge of other texts? The concept of intertextuality will not be unfamiliar to secondary school readers because popular television shows like *Seinfeld* make many intertextual connections to other television and cinematic texts, including *Schindler's List* and the O.J. Simpson trial. A deconstructive approach to reading emphasizes the ways that texts are intertwined and related to one another. Often young readers think that a poetic text is as incomprehensible as if it were written in an unknown language, but reading a poem might require referring to encyclopedic sources of mythology, religion, literature, and history. To read a poem with attention to its intertextual relationships is to be constantly reminded that a poem comprises an inexhaustible convergence of influences. Above all, poets do not write their poems out of the clear air or the inspired imaginations of genius. Poets write out of their personal and cultural knowledge, just as readers read out of their personal and cultural knowledge. In the following poem a deconstructive reading opens up the poem in intriguing ways by paying attention to the way the poem weaves intertextually its braid of connections.

Eve
by Dorothy Livesay

Beside the highway
at the motel door
    it roots
the last survivor of a pioneer
    orchard
miraculously   still
    bearing.

A thud   another apple falls
    I stoop   and   O
that scent   gnarled   ciderish
    with sun in it

that woody pulp
> for teeth and tongue
> to bite and curl around
that spurting juice
> earth-sweet!

In fifty seconds, fifty summers sweep
> and shake me–
I am alive!   can stand
> up   still
hoarding this apple
> in my hand.

"Eve" can be read as the jubilant utterance of a fifty-year-old woman who enjoys eating a fresh apple, or as an expression of joy as the speaker realizes that life—succulent, sun-drenched, earth-sweet life—survives the progression of years, or as a reflection on heritage and roots. A reader might adopt any one (or all) of these stances. But the reader might also read the poem intertextually. As Leonard Orr explains,

> no literary text is written in a vacuum. Besides the general
> culture surrounding the text and the author's own horizon
> (i.e., his experiences, prejudices, use of the language system,
> "worldview," and so on), there are, perhaps more importantly,
> other texts, especially literary texts. (Orr, 1986, 814)

As the word suggests, "intertextuality" refers to the ways a text intersects with other texts and incorporates references to other texts. Because most students are young and usually not widely read, they will not identify many intertextual relations. Nevertheless, they need to be aware of the notion for their reading, and in a poem like "Eve" the intertextuality is not difficult to recognize. The references to Eve and an apple recall the biblical story of Adam and Eve in the Garden of Eden. If students are unfamiliar with the narrative, it ought to be read because by relating that story to the story of the poem, the possibilities for meaning-making are extended. The biblical story is about a beginning and perfection and disobedience and punishment. It is about the Fall and original sin. At least that is how some people in the twentieth-century western world read the story. Others read it as the act of a liberated woman who boldly disobeyed a masculine and tyrannical God. However the narrative is read, Eve survived outside the Garden of Eden and not only survived but became the mother of the human race. Out of the Fall came life on the earth. The speaker of the poem is like a modern Eve, proud and inspired by the ancient Eve.

The following poem is about a photographic pose and the narrator's interpretation of the pose. The reader cannot see the photograph that the narrator refers to, and will tend to accept the narrator's representation of the unseen photograph, but that is the kind of closure that a deconstructive reading defers in order to examine multiple possibilities for interpretation. Students should be asked to explore the poem by putting to work the various strategies for poetic deconstruction that have been provided in this chapter.

Pose
by Zoë Landale

Here we are arranged
into set-pieces on the sofa.
Manners by mother,
& temper by Dad.
Fear all our own.

I am fourteen, the eldest.
I sit with one knee
crossed, hands held in the lap
in closed, palm-on-palm gesture that says
Oh really?
We three girls have put on
hauteur for the camera,
formally assumed mouths
though the youngest's socks
have collapsed at her ankles like panting dogs
& her skirt bunches at the waist.

Our brother gazes at something invisible
on the shag rug.
His downed white lids
give him the look of someone asleep
or dreaming of stillness,
a lizard
lit green glass on a sunny wall.
Somewhere far
from here.
Far from the shouting that will resume
within moments after the *snick*
of the shutter.

The middle girl has round
cheeks & eyes that narrow warily.
She whirls
from one locus of strong emotion
to the next, a compass needle
pulled by forces
for which she has no name.
She will die
when she is twenty without
a word.
In the photograph, she looks guilty
already.

The following comments and questions present possible guides for reading Zoë Landale's "Pose" deconstructively, as well as several suggestions for exercises for creative projects linked to the poem.

Self-Referentiality
How is a poem different from a photograph? How are they similar? Who took the photograph? Who is arranging and watching the pose as the photograph is taken?

Reading from Different Positions

The poem presents the narrator's perspective on a photograph. What textual evidence reveals the narrator's perspective? What perspectives might be presented by the father, or the mother, or the sisters, or the brother?

The narrator is interpreting a photograph of children from the vantage point of an adult. How does memory influence autobiographical writing? How might the narrator as a fourteen-year-old girl have interpreted the photograph? How does time influence memories and perspectives? What is autobiography? What is the relationship between the stories presented in the poem and the stories lived by the family in their daily experiences? What is the relationship between the photograph and the poem? What is the relationship between fiction and truth? How is the "I" as a fourteen-year-old in the photograph related to the "I" who is describing and narrating the photograph?

How does a photograph frame a moment of time in time? What does the word "pose" mean? How does it relate to words like "suppose," "expose," "repose," "dispose," and "position"? How does Landale's "Pose" extend beyond the frame of a photograph?

What adjectives might describe the tone of the narrator's voice in the poem?

Binary Oppositions

How does the narrator develop the opposition between the fiction of the "pose" and the reality of the family's lived experiences? How is the contrast between the mother's manners and the father's temper used to construct a sense of tight tension in the poem? Based on the textual evidence of the poem, what are the oppositions that operate in the poem? In what ways does the narrator present each of the characters in the poem as estranged from all the others, straining to be elsewhere?

How does the version of family presented in the poem differ from the version of family presented in many television situation comedies and dramas?

Figurative/Literal Language

In what ways are "the youngest's socks . . . collapsed at her ankles like panting dogs"? How would real panting dogs in the photograph change the image of the pose? In what ways are the brother and a lizard alike? What are the connotations of the word "lizard"? In what ways is the middle girl like a compass? Does the middle girl's whirling from one strong emotion to another suggest accurately the uncertain direction of the whole family?

As the narrator indicates in the description of herself, "I sit with one knee/crossed, hands held in the lap/in closed, palm-on-palm gesture that says/Oh really?," nothing in the photograph is "real." The photograph presents an illusion, a pose, a position, which can be deconstructed by interpreting the figurative images of the photograph with attention to the literal contexts of the family. Of course, the poem is also one more figurative pose which can be deconstructed by asking why the narrator is so intent on deconstructing the images of the photograph. What are her motives in the poem? How does she use language to deconstruct the images of the photograph at the same time that she constructs new images in her poem? Also, though the oppositions between the images of the family photograph and the lived experiences of the family are presented as stark, there is also a good deal of constraint in the poem. Is the narrator still posing?

A photograph is a still, silent image. What evidence is given in the poem that the narrator's family knows silence intimately? What images appeal to the sense of hearing? In what ways is the poem a breaking of the silence?

Intertextuality

The poem conjures up the long tradition of family portraits in photography, fiction, film, biography, and poetry. There is a genre of the family portrait constructed by Norman Rockwell, and Bill Cosby, and "Leave It to Beaver," and *Reader's Digest* in which the family is presented as sacred, romanticized, and nurturing. In what ways does Landale's poem support and subvert that tradition? There is also a growing emphasis in contemporary fiction and film to present the family in diverse images, to confront the positive and the negative stories of families. In what ways does Landale's poem support and subvert this new emphasis?

Here are a few suggestions for classroom exercises.

ACTIVITIES

1. Compare Zoë Landale's "Pose" to Margaret Atwood's "This Is a Photograph of Me." In small groups students can create dramatic tableaux which present their interpretation of the scene described in the poem. Or in small groups they can create tableaux that present the whole scene around the image of the photograph, including the parents.

2. Students can dramatize and film the scene leading up to the taking of the photograph and the scene which follows taking the photograph.

3. Students can investigate the images of families presented on television.

4. Students can construct a collage of images that depict families.

5. Students can look at photographs of their families and write about the images they see in the photographs.

6. Students can write about memories of their families, and then ask others in their family to compare their memories of the incidents.

7. In order to explore connections between the visual and the verbal, students can write responses to photographs of their families. Next they can ask colleagues who do not know their families well to write responses to the photographs. Then they can compare the responses.

There was a time in my teaching when I would have felt very uncomfortable with these kinds of approaches to reading poetry, especially ones that ask students to deconstruct the family, but I do not want to pretend that reading a poem is a simple activity. Instead I want to acknowledge the complicated dynamics involved in responding to poetry because only then will readers, young and old, know the power of poetry to inform our experiences as individuals who live in community with one another.

In chapter 5, "Cultural Criticism," I present several perspectives and observations that provide a wider context for incorporating the discussions that take place in the other sections of the book. In this final chapter, I do my best to connect all of the theoretical perspectives and practical strategies discussed earlier to the broad contexts of the socio-political and cultural worlds we live in.

Cultural Criticism

Cultural criticism proposes that poetry is a cultural production, and that the relationships between texts and writers and readers are informed and constituted by the cultures in which texts and writers and readers circulate. The focus of this book has been on a reader-response orientation to reading poetry in which readers respond to poems out of their personal experiences and emotions and convictions. While I enthusiastically support the value of inviting readers to respond to poems in personal ways, I do not want to promote the limiting expectation that all that is important in the relationship of the text and the reader is the reader's personal and idiosyncratic identification with the poems. By interacting with poems in personal ways only, readers will likely perpetuate their views of the world, instead of interrogating those views. Readers need to attend to the ways social, economic, political, ethical, and cultural realities are constructed and sustained. A cultural-criticism orientation to reading poetry focuses on issues of gender, class, ethnicity, religion, economic status, sexual orientation, nationality, political conviction, race, age, and ability, and helps students recognize that they always read from particular ideological orientations.

Reading for and against Ideology

In addition to the assumptions readers bring to the reading of a poem regarding what a poem is, how a poem produces effects, and how a poem ought to be read, readers also bring to reading a poem a set of values and beliefs and views about the world and human experience and relationships among people. This understanding comprises part of the reader's ideology about society and culture and history. Ideological assumptions and practices and views about poetry and society always guide a student's reading. In addition, a poetic text is also constrained by ideology, including the rules and conventions that the text uses, as well as the views and assumptions about what is "natural" or appropriate for the culture represented in the text. The act of reading a poem is then the production of meaning that occurs when the reader's ideological perspectives and the text's ideological perspectives come together. Poetry often challenges our ideological perspectives by revealing how hidden and taken-for-granted our perspectives often are and by introducing us to new ones.

I began this book with the question, What is a poem? My goal was to shake up some of the misconceptions that readers frequently bring to the experience of responding to poetry in order to expand our notions about what a poem is and can be. I recall vividly one retired English teacher indignantly instructing me that a poem is an eloquent use of language to express lofty emotions and themes. I agreed with her, but I added that a poem is still babble and doodle. Just recently I told a class that a poem can be about anything, and one student became irate as he defended his personal conviction that a poem should deal only with grand ideas and emotions. I agreed with him, but I still claimed that poetry cannot be confined to a few personal convictions. Teachers need to assist their students in seeking to understand their convictions and experiences in relation to the convictions and experiences of others. That seeking is at the heart of the pedagogical enterprise of English language arts education.

The proposal of alternative strategies for reading and teaching poetry necessarily entails fundamental assumptions about the practices and the functions of schools in general and English curriculum and instruction more specifically. For eight years I taught in high schools that operated with a conservative religious world view. The philosophical foundation supporting my own ambitions and actions as a teacher was crystallized by a critical response to my efforts in a poetry class where I had read a poem by a teenager who had committed suicide. One student asked, "If a person commits suicide, will that person still go to heaven?" It was the kind of question students had posed numerous times, a question of personal relevance to young people taught by parents and church that all religious questions have answers. I hesitated. Finally I replied, "I hope that a loving and merciful God will accept into heaven a person who becomes so depressed he or she takes his or her own life." Before long, I was summoned before a committee of church leaders and principals to discuss the charge that I taught erroneous views in my classes. It was alleged that I had undermined the philosophy of the school by suggesting that suicide was permissible. In the school committee meeting I was reminded that suicide is a sin. Moreover, it was remarked that I was unwise to encourage young people in speculative discussion: they needed to be taught truths.

As a result of this touchstone incident, my views about school—its purposes, functions, relationships—have undergone a critical evaluation. The members of the school committee who examined me believe that a school is a God-ordained extension of the home and the church, all three responsible for educating children holistically—mentally, physically, emotionally, and spiritually. In practical terms this means that all facets of the school experience must be monitored and regulated in order to guarantee that the conservative religious world view is pre-eminently espoused, defended, and adopted. The purpose is the production of conservative religious believers.

Out of this watershed event in my own teaching experience has developed an affinity for the views of educators devoted to cultural criticism. Henry Giroux asks "How can we make schooling meaningful so as to make it critical and how can we make it critical so as to make it emancipatory?" (Giroux, 1981, 34) Giroux proposes that the primary concern of educators is "to address the crucial educational issue of what it means to teach students to think critically, to learn how to affirm their own experiences, and to understand the need to struggle individually and collectively for a more just society." (39)

Cultural theorists have redefined the notion of ideology, and in their redefinition they have expanded the parameters of critical concern about the relationship of ideology to literature and to education. The common understanding of ideology is that it refers to a world view. Therefore, in a poem readers are expected to note (perhaps paraphrase) the poet's world view. In some classes teachers seeking a more personal response might engage in discussion about the similarities and the differences between the world views of the poet and the reader. Cultural theorists have challenged the conventional notion of ideology. Pierre Macherey emphasizes that ideology is not "a system of ideas" but the "material objective practices which participate effectively in the development of material life." (Macherey, 1977, 43) In other words, each one of us is ideologically shaped by the dynamic processes of family and religion and media and government and law and school. Catherine Belsey defines ideology succinctly as "a way of thinking, speaking, experiencing." (Belsey, 1980, 5) Through social and cultural and political institutions such as the church, the school, the media, the family, the legal system (what Louis Althusser calls the ideological state apparatuses), people are introduced into powerfully determined ways of seeing and believing. Reading poetry from the perspectives of cultural criticism provides opportunities for teachers and students to interrogate their lived experiences, their values and beliefs, and to resist narrow parameters that promote ideological homogeneity by excluding diversity.

Ideology relates not only to the practice of reading poetry and the content of poetry, but also to the form of poetry. For example, to a modern reader it is perhaps hard to imagine the stranglehold that the convention of iambic pentameter has exercised on English poetry. Until the turn of this century almost all English poetry from the early Renaissance was written in iambic pentameter. The practice was justified by heated argument that the iambic pentameter line matched felicitously the pattern of the English language. Not unlike Cinderella's ugly stepsisters who insisted that the glass shoe fit their feet when it obviously did not, the effort to squeeze the English language into iambic pentameter often proved only that the language did not fit the pattern. Many of the best-known poets in English developed variations of, or did not use, iambic pentameter. Andrew Marvell used iambic tetrameter. John Donne used a rhythm so blatantly variable that Ben Jonson suggested he ought to be hanged. Those poets who most assiduously obeyed the dictates of iambic pentameter, like Sir Philip Sidney in "Astrophel and Stella," are now frequently regarded as monotonous. Antony Easthope observes that "promoted into dominance by the new courtly culture, pentameter is an historically constituted institution. It is not natural to English poetry but is a specific cultural phenomenon, a discursive form." (Easthope, 1983, 55) Easthope describes how iambic pentameter gained ascendancy over accentual metre because iambic pentameter derives from the valorized classical model of Greek and Latin literature. In other words, English poets wanted to ape the sounds of other languages which they believed were more sophisticated and "properly poetic." (64-65) Free verse, then, represents a break with tradition, a liberation from conventions with pervasive ideological connections. Poetry is always pushing against boundaries and expanding the parameters of possibility.

What can the teacher of secondary school English gain from cultural critics? In a general way the teacher can learn what Giroux knows, that "power, knowledge, ideology, and schooling are linked in ever-changing patterns of complexity." (Giroux, 1981, 104) More specifically, the teacher can learn, like Phil Grierson and Chris Richardson, to demystify the phenomenon of language itself, and that "this demystification needs to be accompanied by an examination, both historical and social, of the relationship between people, their languages, and the world in which they live." (Grierson and Richardson, 1982, 15) And most importantly the teacher can learn to follow John Willinsky's advice: "I ask that student and teacher look up from the literature anthology, from their private and shared responses, to study how the poem is part of a larger literate enterprise. It means taking field trips that relentlessly trace the text out into the world." (Willinsky, 1990, 190) Equipped with a new perspective the teacher's task will be no easier (indeed, it will likely be more demanding), but it will be more effective, and subsequently more rewarding for everyone.

In addition, teachers need to interrogate their methodology because behind that methodology lurks ideology, and unexamined, unacknowledged ideology is a source of blindness. What criteria guide your selection of poetry? Do you use only the poetry of the "high cultural tradition"? Do you use the poetry of popular culture—lyrics of songs, sentiments on Carlton cards, advertising jingles, found poems? Are you eager that your students learn the important truth of the poem, or that they explore their perceptions of the world? Do you examine your own world with your students? As teachers become more reflexive about their practices in the classroom they must also examine the basic assumptions that undergird their practices. They must examine what they are attempting to teach and why they are attempting to teach it. Are your goals significant?

And they must guide their students (by their example) into their own reflexive questioning: In what ways does this poem exercise power over the reader? How does this poem affect readers? What are the contexts in which the poem was written? How do the contexts for reading the poem affect the ways it is read? From what positions can it be read? Does a woman read the poem differently from a man? Antony Easthope suggests that "any text, especially one such as a poem, is constantly read and re-read in different ways by different people, by the same people at different times in their lives, by different people at different periods in history." (Easthope, 1983, 18) The term "cultural criticism" refers generically to a wide range of perspectives that are focussed on the ideological dynamics of culture, history, politics, and society, but in order for teachers and readers of poetry in the secondary school to use successfully the approaches of cultural criticism, they need specific advice. Therefore, this chapter is divided into several sections which discuss and illustrate five perspectives of cultural criticism: historicism, Marxism, feminism, post-colonialism, and race. These five perspectives are not necessarily discrete; they intersect one another in many ways. Historicism addresses issues of historical context, and demonstrates how history is a story written by people, a crafted and interpreted version of events, always open for further retelling and interpretation. Marxism focusses on how institutions, like school, church, government, and business, shape the ways that people live, think, believe, and relate in the world. Feminism addresses issues of the cultural production of gender identities, and interrogates inequities constructed around gender differences. Post-colonialism addresses and revisits relationships between nations of the world where some nations have been colonizers and others have been colonized. Finally, race focusses attention on the ways that political and economic power have been divided up inequitably among different races, and how these inequities are propagated and perpetuated.

Historicism

A poem is the product of history. Written in a particular place and time, it is motivated and constrained by the historical conditions of the place and time in which it was initially written and read, as well as all subsequent places and times, including the present conditions of the reading.

Terry Eagleton notes succinctly that "to understand literature . . . means understanding the total social process of which it is part." (Eagleton, 1976, 6) Digging into the historical background, and relating a poem to the present historical context are time-consuming activities, but the time will be well spent.

In order to illustrate the usefulness of considering the historical contexts of a poem, read the following poem written by an anonymous girl in the Terezin concentration camp in 1941.

Birdsong

He doesn't know the world at all

Who stays in his nest and doesn't go out.
He doesn't know what birds know best
Nor what I want to sing about,
That the world is full of loveliness.

When dewdrops sparkle in the grass
And earth's aflood with morning light,
A blackbird sings upon a bush
To greet the dawning after night.
Then I know how fine it is to live.

Hey, try to open up your heart
To beauty; go to the woods someday
And weave a wreath of memory there.
Then if the tears obscure your way
You'll know how wonderful it is

To be alive.

It is certainly possible to read this poem with no more information than that already provided, to read it with an emotional response, a heightened identification with the sentiments of the poem. But how much more memorable and instructive will the experience of the poem be if the teacher provides opportunities for reading about the concentration camps of World War II? No adolescent will quickly forget Elie Wiesel's account of the concentration camps in *Night*. Or how many students have read or seen *Sophie's Choice* or *Schindler's List*? What have they read in history class? Does this poem acquire a larger significance because of its historical context? Is the poem in its anonymity the earnest cry of millions of people who were slaughtered because of a conflict in ideologies? Perhaps the class could spend the entire year studying the historical contexts of the poem; a facetious proposal, of course, but, nevertheless, a possible one because when the class has read a hundred books on World War II, they can always read a hundred more that chronicle the concentration camps of the present age—the Gulag Archipelago or the prison camps of Chile, for example.

Marxism

Schools and university English departments have typically perpetuated misconceptions regarding poetry as élitist and culturally sophisticated and exclusionary. In the 1970s I went to the chair of the Department of English at Memorial University of Newfoundland to discuss a subject for a graduate thesis. I told him that I wanted to write a thesis on a Newfoundland poet. He smiled and asked, "Who would want to read it?", and I chose instead to write on a minor British poet. Every poem—integrally connected to the social, historical, political, cultural, and economic contexts in which writers, readers, publishers, booksellers, teachers, curriculum designers, and administrators operate—is imbued with the ideological contexts of its inception, its transmission, and its reception. In his compelling essay, "Democratizing Literature: Issues in Teaching Working-Class Literature," Nicholas Coles argues that the history of English literature and criticism has privileged one kind of literature, "the obscure and highly wrought," "while the literature of women, of Black, ethnic, and working-class writers–of most people, in other words–was excluded or admitted only by exception, in a form of discrimination that, at bottom, has less to do with valuations of literary quality than with the social distribution of power." (Coles, 1986, 665) Readers need to be able to interrogate issues of distribution of power. A poem is not an ethereal or esoteric use of language; a poem is a verbal artifact construed and constructed by flesh-and-blood writers and flesh-and-blood readers with their feet solidly rooted in the world. Gerald Gregory proposes in "Community-published Working-class Writing in Context" that:

> a fresh, democratic sense of print and books as available, stripped of authority and false dignity, written by flesh-and-blood people with particular points of view and purposes, and, therefore, susceptible of reply and rebuttal as well as respect and reverence . . . is self-evidently and powerfully educational. (Gregory, 1094, 228)

In 1994 I published a book of poems titled *Growing Up Perpendicular on the Side of a Hill*. The collection deals with the ordinary experiences of growing up on Lynch's Lane in Corner Brook, Newfoundland. I began the collection when I was about thirty-four years old. In the collection I write about people and experiences that I never wrote about in school where I tried to mimic the writing I read in class anthologies. For years and years I heard an insistent voice of warning that it is not sufficient to write poetry about ordinary people. As a boy in school I did not think it was legitimate to write about the kinds of stories that I lived daily. Who would be interested in the lives of ordinary people? Poetry, I was convinced, was about famous people and grand adventures and lofty ideas and intense emotions. I grew up with a clear, strong sense that poetry had no connection to my daily lived experiences, and my teachers, instructed and constructed by school textbooks and guidebooks, sustained and perpetuated the separation. During an interview a newspaper reporter asked me about *Growing Up Perpendicular on the Side of a Hill*. "The people in your poems are very strange," he said. "Are they real or did you make them up?" I replied that the people I had grown up with were a lot stranger than the characters in my poems. The newspaper reporter who used the word "strange" to describe the characters in my poems was responding out of his sense of unfamiliarity with the experiences and emotions presented. The world conjured in the poems is unfamiliar because the working-class world of a mill town in Newfoundland has been significantly excluded from poetry. It is a strange world because it is unknown, and it is unknown, at least in part, because it has not been perceived as an appropriate subject for poetry. The title *Growing Up Per-*

pendicular on the Side of a Hill suggests paradoxically a living experience of right angles and vertiginous imbalance which acknowledges the tangled, complicated stories people live. As a student in school I did not write about the kinds of stories told in *Growing Up Perpendicular on the Side of a Hill,* and I did not read about these kinds of stories. But the poetry classroom is a site where students and teachers can read and write about the "strange" and the "unfamiliar" as they interrogate the ways that the world is ideologically constructed and seek together ways to create new possibilities for knowing the world.

The following poem about ordinary people and ordinary lives contributes to the poetic tradition of exploring the experiences of people from different class backgrounds. It nevertheless takes a provocative approach to that tradition (does it really honour people by recording narratives of mutilation, madness, alcohol and drug abuse, death, adultery, vandalism, violence, and unfulfilled talents?). Teachers might use it to explore a poem from a Marxist perspective while questioning what a Marxist perspective accomplishes.

Growing Up Perpendicular on the Side of a Hill
by Carl Leggo

in a house hammered into a hill hanging over
the Humber Arm I grew up and watched the cargo
ships come and go without me through spring
summer autumn winter and watched Ro Carter
open the shutters on his store where
everything you ever needed could be bought and
listened for the mill steam whistle announcing
the hours and disasters always whistling

and at sixteen I left 7 Lynch's Lane Corner
Brook Newfoundland and I've been leaving for
more than two decades never staying anywhere
long enough to get to know people well enough
to have a fight an argument even and perhaps
all this time I've been running away from

Lynch's Lane where I lived a soap opera with
no commercial breaks and grew up perpendicular
on the side of a hill

with Gordie Gorman whose mother one Christmas
gave him a hunting knife with a blade like a
silver bell but Gordie Gorman refused to carve
the turkey and hunted through the house with
one clean slice down to the side cut off his
penis instead and was rushed to Montreal where
it was sewed back on though neighbours said it
never worked right again and Gordie Gorman
said only I wanted to see how sharp it was

and Francie Baker who spent a whole year in
bed just woke up on New Year's Day and said
I'm not getting up this year and day after day
just lay in bed reading the newspaper and
looking out the window and she always waved at
Cec Frazer Macky my brother and me when we
climbed the crab tree to watch her

and Tommy Stuckless the midget who we all gave
nickels to do hand-stands and somersaults and
was fierce and cranky like a crackie dog and
ran off to Toronto and became a wrestler

and Frankie Sheppard who disappeared during
his high school graduation and was found three
days later in the trees near Wild Cove mute
with the stories aswirl around his head LSD
and Old Niagara and rock music and his
girlfriend's mother finding him pinched
between her daughter's legs like a lobster

and Mikey Bishop who stopped everybody on the
road flashed open his black overcoat never
without it want to buy a watch hundreds of
watches pinned to the inside of the coat the
only thing ticking about Mikey Bishop said Cec

and Bonnie Winsor who rubbed herself with
coconut oil and lay on a red blanket in her
underwear like a movie star between sheets of
tin foil toasting in the spring sun and
sometimes smiled at Cec Frazer Macky my
brother and me hiding in the tall grass
watching her turning and cooking like a
chicken on a spit and we asked her if we could
take Polaroid snaps and she said yes but by
the time we saved up enough money for film
summer was over and Bonnie Winsor's brown body
was hidden away for another year

and Bertie Snooks who joined the army got a
haircut flew to Cornwallis and was run over by
a sergeant in a jeep without meeting the enemy
even before he completed basic training

and Sissy Fudge who was the smartest girl in
Harbourview Academy and could have been a
lawyer or doctor or engineer but had her first
baby at fifteen and almost one a year for the
next decade or two like a friggin' Coke
machine said Macky

and Janie Berkshire who built a big two-story
house with her husband Pleaman and the night
Cec Frazer Macky my brother and I carried and
dragged Pleaman all the way up Old Humber Road
and Lynch's Lane from the Caribou Tavern where

107

he sometimes went after prayer meetings at the
Glad Tidings Tabernacle Janie Berkshire threw
Pleaman out the new plate glass window and he
fell two stories buried in snow and Cec Frazer
Macky my brother and I hid Pleaman in Cec's
basement for the night and Janie Berkshire
painted the house magenta and raised three
daughters and served tea and walnut sandwiches
at weekly meetings with the women of Lynch's
Lane but wouldn't let Pleaman Berkshire or any
other man in the house again

and Denney Winsor whose wife ran off with an
optometrist and Denney started lifting weights
in order to beat the shit out of the
optometrist but enjoyed weightlifting so much
he shaved all the hair off his legs and chest
and came third in the Mr. Corner Brook
Bodybuilding Contest

and Sammy Sheppard who turned sixteen and
didn't want to be a boy scout or a missionary
or an honours student or a star basketball
player and took his father's lead mallet and
smashed up seven of the concrete benches at
Margaret Bowater Park until he couldn't lift
the mallet over his head anymore and spent a
few weeks in the Whitburne Detention and
Reform Center for Juveniles where he was a
model inmate

and Louella Skiffington who always wore her
fuchsia dress to the Glad Tidings Tabernacle
every Sunday and Wednesday night and for
special prayer meetings I'm devoted to the
soul-saving business she said until she came

home early one night ill and found Ronnie
Skiffington singing hymns with Amanda Parsons
the choir director and Louella stopped wearing
her fuchsia dress stopped going to the Glad Tidings
Tabernacle parked her old life like a
car wreck in the backyard and most nights
brought Greek and Portuguese second mates home
from the Caribou Tavern still saving souls the
neighbours said

but for all my running away I never escape
Lynch's Lane like the weather always mad
spring under a moon always full bonfire summer
autumn ablaze winter without end the hill
where I grew up perpendicular

Reading poetry from Marxist perspectives is unsettling because Marxism challenges "reality" as we know it, opens up a dizzying array of possibilities, and interrogates the ways power is distributed among people. Above all, a Marxist reading of a poem precludes closure by encouraging questions, in the way of the following exercises.

ACTIVITY
Do your students know people in real life or other characters in film or TV or stories like the characters in "Growing Up Perpendicular on the Side of a Hill"? They may want to discuss the similarities.

ACTIVITY
Does "Growing Up Perpendicular on the Side of a Hill" simply perpetuate stereotyped views of the working class or does the poem contribute to interrogating the ways that class constructs and constrains identities for people?

ACTIVITY
Have students investigate the narrator's claim in "Growing Up Perpendicular on the Side of a Hill": "I lived a soap opera with/no commercial

breaks." What does it mean to "live a soap opera"? What are the conventions of a soap opera? Have students compare the poem to popular soap operas. In what ways are the poem and the conventional soap opera alike?

ACTIVITY

How reliable is the narrator in "Growing Up Perpendicular on the Side of a Hill"? Can your students trust the narrator's stories? What are the relations between the narrator and the characters? Have your students imagine that they are characters in the poem, and have them write other poems or stories in which they write back to the narrator objecting to the way they are depicted, and revising the account of their stories.

ACTIVITY

Do your students find any of the stories in the poem inappropriate for reading in a secondary school class? Your students may want to discuss their reservations and the reasons why they deem a particular story inappropriate, or they may want to offer arguments for why no story should be considered inappropriate.

ACTIVITY

Have your students discuss the narrator's claim, "for all my running away I never escape/Lynch's Lane."

ACTIVITY

As a class your students can compile an anthology of poetry about different lived experiences. Each student can contribute one poem that represents a part of his or her personal experience.

ACTIVITY

How do cultural artifacts like clothing, food, cars, and music help to define the identities of people? If your students could include one item in a time capsule to be opened a hundred years from now, what would the object be? Why?

ACTIVITY

Have your students select a day of the week that they anticipate will be an ordinary day, and have them keep a detailed diary of all the events and encounters and emotions that they experience in that ordinary day. What comprises "an ordinary day"? How does their ordinary day differ from the ordinary day of one of their classmates? How do we define "ordinariness"?

ACTIVITY

Have students collect local poems or stories about working and the workplace from family, friends, and neighbours.

ACTIVITY

How do your students believe class is represented in popular culture? In other words, what are the features that mark or distinguish one class from another? Your students may want to reconsider bill bissett's "th wundrfulness uv th mountees our secret police" as an example of a poem that challenges notions of class identity. In what ways is bissett's use of phonetic spelling instead of conventional spelling liberating for writers and readers? How and why does bissett's innovative language use contribute to his interrogation of the distribution of power among people?

ACTIVITY

Have your students survey people in their neighbourhoods regarding their past and current experiences with poetry. Have them investigate the role of poetry in contemporary society. Who reads poetry? How popular is poetry? How accessible is poetry? What are our attitudes about poetry?

Feminism

I have known a keen sense of exclusion when reading poetry which ignores my working-class experience, but I can only begin to imagine the sense of exclusion women must feel when they read the literature sanctioned for use in schools. In *What's Wrong With High School English? ... It's Sexist Un-Canadian Outdated,* published in 1980, Priscilla Galloway reports the results of an extensive survey of English courses in Ontario high schools. Among her conclusions she reveals that typical messages about women communicated in the courses include:

- Women are less important than men, as participants in fictional worlds and societies and as creators of them.
- Women follow the leadership of men.
- For women, the domestic role emerges as the norm: wife and/or mother. This is true even of the rare women who have jobs, and the even more rare ones with careers. Women are seen in relation to men, but men are often seen in relation to other men, in various aspects of their careers or jobs or quests.
- Physical beauty of a modest kind is equated with appropriately "womanly" virtue; sensuality in a woman is coupled with evil or with triviality.
- The value of a woman is determined by men rather than by other women; women's relationships with other women, where they exist, are less important than relationships with men.
- When women are heroic, they are heroic as sufferers, rather than as people of action.
- Women tend to be romantic and impractical; men attend to the work of the world.
- Women show themselves ready to abandon their own priorities, to sacrifice themselves/their happiness, and their lives for men. (Galloway, 1980, 85-86)

Galloway recommends that "requirements for balance in the curriculum must include male-female balance, of authors and of protagonists, in order that the stated objectives for personal growth may be made realistically attainable for female students as well as for males." (122) More than a decade after Galloway, I conducted a research project in 1993 in which I investigated the English literature curriculum resources used in British Columbia secondary schools. I examined more than two hundred texts authorized and recommended for use in English literature courses in grades eight to twelve. I examined these texts in order to compare the number of items written by women and the number of items written by men, and to compare the images of women and men revealed in the texts. Very little has changed since Galloway's study. A comparison of the number of poems written by women and the number of poems written by men reveals that women are significantly underrepresented as authors. Out of a total of 1,498 poems in the school anthologies only 236 poems are written by women (that is, sixteen percent). As English educators we need to ask the following questions: What criteria do we use when making decisions about the literature that we teach? How well read are we in the writing of women? Are the canonical works of English literature mostly written by men because women don't write, or because writing by women has been ignored by patriarchal institutions of publishing and distribution and reviewing and scholarship?

Not only are women underrepresented as authors in the literature used in secondary schools, but women are typically presented as subservient, submissive, supportive, sexy, sensitive, self-conscious, security-seeking, shallow, and soft-hearted sources of succour. Women are presented again and again in ways that reinforce stereotypes. Frequently women have no role at all—they are totally invisible. It is not often that a text includes no male characters. Women are often presented in cruel and violent ways. Women are generally presented in the context of the family. Seldom are women presented independent of relationships with men. In general terms, they perform roles of service and nurturance. Their professional careers are limited to teaching and nursing. Women's roles seem so much more restrictive than men's. Generally, the world seems preoccupied with men's needs. Men apparently run the world, and the world apparently revolves around men at the centre of commerce, politics, industry, law, and education. At the same time, men are almost exclusively presented in narrow terms as abusive, evil, combative, violent, proud, competitive, selfish, adventuresome, estranged, and solitary.

Some questions that students need to be encouraged to ask concerning the images of women and men include the following: Why are women so seldom seen in roles of adventure, daring, leadership, courage? Why are women so often seen as introspective and reflective and sensitive while men are seldom seen this way? Why are women frequently presented in negative ways? Why are women seldom presented in positions of money and power? Where are the texts that present the life experiences of women and men in all their multiplicity?

I agree with Elaine Showalter that we need "a new universal literary history and criticism that combines the literary experiences of both women and men, a complete revolution in the understanding of our literary heritage." (Showalter, 1986, 10) Lately I have begun to focus my reading attention on books by women. It is time to rectify the common perception created by school textbooks that there is only a limited number of women writers. In fact there are thousands of women writers whose voices can be heard across centuries and countries if only we are willing to listen. How many of us know Kate Braid, di brandt, P.K. Page, Elizabeth Brewster, Phyllis McGinley, Tess Gallagher, Erin Mouré, or Martha Hillhouse? It will be a long time before I run out of women authors to read. *The Feminist Companion to Literature in English* includes more than 2,700 biographic and bibliographic entries on women writers. There are thousands of women poets whose voices can be heard across centuries and countries if only we are willing to listen. Teachers and students need opportunities to read poetry that is genuinely representative of the wide range of experiences that women and men live.

Consider the following poem:

Checking the Doors
by Renee Norman

i open the car door and climb into the back seat
a cane lies across the floor
it hooks me in
my father has parked in the handicapped spot
a tag on the rearview mirror announces this new privilege

my mother looks over her shoulder as he drives
reads out road signs   gives warnings
      checks traffic flow
they banter back and forth
with the intimacy 47 years develops
my father snaps at my mother
when she makes one suggestion too many
and she grows cold and silent
the air crisp with belittlement
    and impatience
      change

114

my father makes his way to the front door
slowly with the cane
my mother and i carry in my suitcases
and he goes up to bed to rest
my mother solicitous about his pain
playing roles i am unaccustomed to viewing

my father forgets to lock the doors at night sometimes,
she tells me over tea
and it isn't so easy for her to leave anymore
he likes to complain to her, she adds
and gets tired now
a bowl of soup fills him

my father forgets to lock the doors at night,
my mother repeats to me
she has to check them herself
she listens for the one on the garage to close
when he's been out playing cards

who will check the doors when *i* get old,
my mother asks
clearing cups
hands marked with liver spots
the flesh on her upper arms
hangs loose like deflated water wings

i do not answer
i am struck dumb by doors flying open and banging shut
the echo of words i could not voice aloud
but wish i had:
    i will check them when you get old, mother
    i will check the doors

Marnie O'Neill suggests that "culturally critical reading practices
have the potential to construct critical readers as opposed to responsive

readers." (O'Neill, 1993, 24) I do not want to set up a binary opposition between "responsive readers" and "critical readers" because critical readers are responsive readers, but there are degrees of difference between reading critically and reading responsively. It is possible to read Norman's "Checking the Doors" as an expression of the narrator's affectionate concern for the aging parents, and the sense of responsibility for caring for aging parents. But a culturally critical reading will interrogate how the poem constructs and is constructed by cultural predispositions that are taken for granted. The poem revolves around a stereotypical relationship between a man and a woman. The mother is concerned that she now has responsibility for the security of the household. The father "forgets to lock the doors at night." The mother wonders who will check the doors when she gets old. A culturally critical reading of the poem reveals how the relationship of the father and the mother is constructed in ways that represent the traditional gendered imbalance of the man who looks after the woman. The picture of the mother and the father as they drive and banter and snap, as they relate in silence and solicitation, is the stuff of popular culture, George's parents on *Seinfeld*, for example. But the energy of the poem is not in the stereotypical representation of an aging couple. There is a twist at work in the poem that can be missed in a reading that concentrates too willingly on the predictable emotions of the story. The second and third lines of the poem, "a cane lies across the floor/it hooks me in," hint at the complex emotions that generate the poem. In my first few readings of "Checking the Doors," I read the final stanza as the narrator's response to her mother's concern about who will check the doors when she gets old. I applauded the narrator's resolution and promise to "check them when you get old, mother." In a way I was hooked by the poem—I read the poem through my own personal presuppositions and desires regarding issues of who cares for the aging. Motivated by a traditional perspective on the importance of extended families and having grown up in a home where my grandmother was an integral part of the family, I read the final stanza as the narrator's promise to care for her mother. From a particular position, then, I read the poem, but my reading is only one of several possible readings. What is interesting in the final stanza is that the narrator does not promise to "check the doors." Instead the narrator is struck dumb by "the echo of words i could not voice aloud/but wish i had:/i will check them when you get old, mother/i will check the doors." The narrator does not actually say the words, only wishes that she had said them, and therein lies the subtle complexity of the poem: responsibility for the aging is no simple responsibility. What are the narrator's motivations and desires?

The poem opens up the complex web of dynamics that constitute contemporary culture and society. "Checking the Doors" constructs a particular version of events and experiences. It would be interesting to have students rewrite the poem from the father's perspective or the mother's perspective. From what positions can readers read the poem? As a reader I was "hooked" into a particular reading position by the tone or voice of the poem, by identification with culturally sanctioned ways of construing the stories of the aging, but by resisting this reading position I open up the possibilities for more wide-ranging readings. I begin to question the cultural expectations about marriage, man-woman relationships, aging, and children's responsibilities. I am "checking the doors" to see what unknown possibilities lie behind them, and the challenge for the high school teacher is to find ways to encourage students to do the same. Feminism reminds teachers and students to "check the doors," to investigate the ways that identities and relationships have been gendered, to interrogate the stereotypes of women's roles and men's roles, to question inequities of power, and to promote possibilities for enhancing women's and men's lived experiences.

ACTIVITY

Have students compile an anthology of favourite poetry by women. Encourage them to seek poetry by women from around the world. Students could compile poetry which foregrounds themes of sex and gender.

ACTIVITY

Have students explore ways in which poetry by women is like and unlike poetry by men. For example, students might select a poem by a woman and a poem by a man, two poems about a similar subject, and print the two poems in parallel columns on a sheet of bristol board. They could then list the similarities and differences in thematic focus, representation of emotions, use of language, poetic structure, and adherence to convention.

In order to pursue further the exploration of gender differences, compare the poetry written by women in the class to the poetry written by men. All members of a class could write poems about the same subject, and then discuss the gender differences revealed in the poems. I am not suggesting that women and men necessarily write differently, or that there is a kind of poetry that only women write and a kind that only men write, but examining differences in poems written by women and men can disclose some of the ways that poetry helps both support and challenge the construction of gender identities.

ACTIVITY

Have students plan a conference around poetry by women with readings, visiting poets, and discussion groups. Some topics for discussion with the visiting poets might include writing habits, reasons for writing, mentors and influences, sources of ideas, choice of subjects, reflections on getting published, and how gender influences their writing and how their writing is responded to.

ACTIVITY

Have students research the biography of a woman poet, and present a collage or a multimedia presentation or a drama about the poet which explores the significance of gender in the poet's life and work.

Have students interview a woman poet. This project could be done in teams of four or five students who will prepare questions to ask the poet and then conduct the interview.

ACTIVITY

Have students find poems written by women about men, and poems written by men about women. For example, *Poetry Alive: Perspectives,* compiled and edited by Dom Saliani, includes "Lucinda Matlock" by Edgar Lee Masters and "Alex" by Phyllis Webb. Most anthologies of poetry will provide useful examples. Have students discuss the issue of whether or not a man can write about a woman's experiences, or a woman about a man's experiences.

ACTIVITY

Have students compile an anthology of poetry by gay and lesbian poets. A consideration of issues of gender raises important questions about how gender identities are constructed and perpetuated. Gay and lesbian poets interrogate conceptions of gender identities. In her collection of poems *Fire Power,* Chrystos explains that "Fire Power is . . . about truth as fire and as power. It is seeing my life as a First Nations Two-Spirited Lesbian as fire & as power which can help heal our mother and ourselves. Poetry is the song of the people, not the painted bird of the academic machine." (Chrystos, 1995,129) Lesbian and gay poetry is fired in political, social, historical, and cultural contexts that disrupt and contravene and question the status quo: seemingly natural ways of living in the world that are taken for granted. When students compile an anthology of poetry by lesbian and gay poets, they can investigate the main themes, the perspectives on experiences, and the ways identities are shaped.

Post-colonialism

The focus of post-colonialism is keenly represented in the title, *The Empire Writes Back: Theory and Practice in Post-Colonial Literatures* by Bill Ashcroft, Gareth Griffiths, and Helen Tiffin. Post-colonial theory and practice revisits and revisions the historical and contemporary relationships between the peoples of colonizer nations and the peoples of colonized nations. A significant question raised by post-colonialism is the question of who has the authority of authorship. By way of example, consider the ways that native peoples are presented in poetry. Around the world native peoples have typically been written in poetry by western colonizers—soldiers, explorers, and entrepreneurs, intent on business and political ventures. What are the images and stories of native peoples presented in these poems? How do these poems construct the identities of native peoples? How do native peoples present themselves in their own words?

Consider the following poem:

119

History Lesson
by Jeannette Armstrong

Out of the belly of Christopher's ship
a mob bursts
Running in all directions
Pulling furs off animals
Shooting buffalo
Shooting each other
left and right

Father mean well
waves his makeshift wand
forgives saucer-eyed Indians

Red coated knights
gallop across the prairie
to get their men
and to build a new world

Pioneers and traders
bring gifts
Smallpox, Seagrams
and rice krispies

Civilization has reached
the promised land

Between the snap crackle pop
of smoke stacks
and multicoloured rivers
swelling with flower powered zee
are farmers sowing skulls and bones
and miners
pulling from gaping holes
green paper faces
of a smiling English lady

The colossi
in which they trust
while burying
breathing forests and fields
beneath concrete and steel
stand shaking fists
waiting to mutilate
whole civilizations
ten generations at a blow

Somewhere among the remains
of skinless animals
is the termination
to a long journey
and unholy search
for the power
glimpsed in a garden
forever closed
forever lost

The following discussion of "History Lesson" illustrates some of the complex dynamics that are generated in a post-colonial reading of a poem. The beginning image of the poem, "Out of the belly of Christopher's ship/a mob bursts," reminds me that one version of the death of Judas Iscariot, the disciple who betrayed Jesus Christ to the military authorities, claims that Judas Iscariot died when he fell on stones and his belly burst. The image is revolting, as is the image of a mob that bursts out of a belly. But is my reading of Armstrong's image accurate or appropriate? I am importing an image from western Judaeo-Christian culture in order to discuss a poem that ostensibly seeks to challenge the hegemony of that culture. Whether appropriate or not, I cannot avoid reading the poem out of my cultural experiences and knowledge. On the other hand, I can grow more reflexive about my grounded positions in cultural contexts. To read Jeanette Armstrong's "History Lesson" post-colonially is to read it with an abiding sense of uneasiness—I cannot close down the meaning-making. While students cannot escape their learned ideological positions, they can learn to resist and interrogate those positions by taking a cue from the narrative voice of the poem.

What is the narrator's voice like in "History Lesson"? After the initial image of a mob bursting out of the ship's belly, the images continue to construct a picture of mayhem: "Running in all directions/Pulling furs off animals/Shooting buffalo/Shooting each other/left and right." The image is ludicrous (conjuring up the zaniness of the Keystone cops), but the relentless litany of violence militates against any laughter. The mob that bursts out of the belly of Christopher's ship violates everything and everyone, even its own members. In my reading, there is no doubting the anger in the narrator's voice. In subsequent stanzas the narrator continues to occupy a rhetorical stance of uncompromising denunciation, even in the second stanza where the language is more subtle: "Father mean well/waves his makeshift wand/forgives saucer-eyed Indians." The sound of "Father mean well" mimics the language of the colonizers as presented in Hollywood films (just consider Tonto in "The Lone Ranger" who always spoke in an ungrammatical idiom that represented his otherness). The colonizer "forgives saucer-eyed Indians"—again the description of Indians as "saucer-eyed" is part of the colonizers' stereotypical description of aboriginal peoples as overwhelmed by the might and knowledge of the colonizers. The narrator plays with the word "forgives"—who needs forgiveness and who can forgive and what are the motives for forgiveness? At every turn there is bold and blatant sarcasm: the police are "Red coated knights" and the pioneers who will "build a new world" bring "gifts" of "Smallpox, Seagrams/and Rice Krispies." Perhaps more than any other image of the poem, the connection between disease and whiskey on the one hand, and Rice Krispies on the other, creates the pervasive sense that the colonizers have brought nothing but destruction. When the woman who invented Rice Krispie squares died recently, newspapers all over North America carried the announcement of her death as well as her recipe for the famous squares. The narrator in Armstrong's poem calls even the seemingly innocuous Rice Krispies into question as a worthwhile contribution: "Between the snap crackle pop/of smoke stacks/and multi-coloured rivers," there can be found only "the termination/to a long journey/and unholy search/for the power/glimpsed in a garden/forever closed/forever lost." The voice in Armstrong's poem is sarcastic, ironic, angry, and compelling. The words are barked between clenched teeth. The colonized is talking back to the colonizer, and the history of moral and military and mercantile imperative which motivated the colonizers is re/presented as a history of greed and violence and self-fulfilling righteousness.

Armstrong's poem does not teach me history as I learned history in school. The poem is angry, and I feel very uneasy when I read it, but that feeling of being unsettled is an integral part of the experience of poetry. When I read Armstrong's poem in a recent class, one English education student responded with a vociferous rejection of the view of history presented in the poem. The student wanted to focus on the benefits that European explorers brought to the New World. Armstrong's poem is sure to raise many divergent points of view; the poem shakes up readers. I think "History Lesson" is an outstanding poem to discuss in school because it highlights the ways that ideology works to create a sense of truth, the way things are. The poem invites readers to investigate the notion that North America was "discovered" by European explorers. What is the history of native people? Who has written the history of native people? How are native people represented in literature and film and television? How are the stories of native people presented in news reports? Armstrong's poem shakes up the long-standing historical tradition of glorifying the discovery and settlement of a continent where people had lived for centuries before Europeans arrived. An investigation of this history illustrates a story of injustice. Without knowing this history most of the current experience of native people will also be misunderstood. I realize that my effort to read "History Lesson" with attention to postcolonial perspectives still represents only one reading. I am not attempting to figure out Jeanette Armstrong's intentions, and I am not seeking to close down the responses of other readers who might choose to read the poem in neutral or dispassionate ways, or politically reactionary ways, or historically conservative ways. I do not want to preclude alternative readings. Perhaps I have read too much into Armstrong's poem with my contention that the narrator's voice is angry. Perhaps the narrator's voice is a voice of dismay or humour or sadness or madness. Nevertheless, I choose to read the poem out of my own cultural experiences and ideological perspectives as a manifesto filled with zeal for revisiting the lessons of history in order to know how to live more successfully in the future. I, therefore, reject a neutral or apolitical reading of the poem in favour of an ideologically and politically charged interpretation. But, above all, I read the poem as an invitation to engage in a conversation with native people and non-native people about how we form and re-form the world. The following exercises are intended to help students and teachers explore poetry from post-colonial perspectives that open up possibilities for seeing the world in renewed ways of justice and fairness.

ACTIVITY

To begin, invite students to ask themselves the kinds of questions that I have asked in my responses to the poem. In other words, how do they respond to the tone of the narrator's voice, and how do they explain their responses to the narrator's voice? What experiences and knowledge determine their responses?

ACTIVITY

Have students examine representations of native men and women in television, films, and advertising and popular magazines. For example, students might compare the representations of native women and men in early television and films with representations in current television and films, as a way of beginning to ask questions like, Who constructs these images? Why are these images constructed? Who benefits from these images? Who does not benefit from these images? How do these images relate to the lived experiences of native men and women?

ACTIVITY

Have students compile an anthology of poetry by native poets. Each student could take responsibility for researching the poetry of one native poet, and then present two poems by the poet for the class anthology. What are the representations of native identities in poetry by native women and men? In other words, how do native poets construct their understanding of their lived experiences in the world? How do these images differ from the images presented in the television, films, advertising, and popular magazines examined in the previous exercise?

ACTIVITY

Have students ask several people in the community to respond to a poem by a native poet, and compare their responses. In this way, students can bring native poetry into the community, as well as experience the range of responses from different members of the community.

ACTIVITY

Invite native poets to visit the classroom to discuss their reasons for writing, their experiences as poets, their choice of subjects, and the responses to their poetry.

ACTIVITY

Compare the poetry of native writers in North America with native writers in Australia or South America. What are the similarities and differences in choice of subjects and development of themes and use of poetic techniques?

ACTIVITY

Research the history of colonialism, and imaginatively recreate scenarios in which peoples from colonizing and colonized nations meet for the first time, and cooperatively plan for a future together.

Issues of Race

Margaret Walker's "For My People" is an appropriate poem to conclude this section on "reading for and against ideology" because, like Jeanette Armstrong, Walker presents a revised and revitalizing view of the history of African-Americans in North America. The poem is written from the point of view of the African-American when North American history has been typically written by white people. Like Armstrong's "History Lesson," Walker's poem is an invitation to revisit the ideological representation of race. It is an unsettling poem, but its lyricism recalls and echoes African-American traditions of music and oratory.

For My People
by Margaret Walker

For my people everywhere singing their slave songs repeat-
    edly: their dirges and their ditties and their blues and
    jubilees, praying their prayers nightly to an unknown
    god, bending their knees humbly to an unseen power;

For my people lending their strength to the years, to the gone
    years and the now years and the maybe years, washing
    ironing cooking scrubbing sewing mending hoeing
    plowing digging planting pruning patching dragging
    along never gaining never reaping never knowing and
    never understanding;

For my playmates in the clay and dust and sand of Alabama
    backyards playing baptizing and preaching and doc-
    tor and jail and soldier and school and mama and
    cooking and playhouse and concert and store and hair
    and Miss Choomby and company;

For the cramped bewildered years we went to school to learn
    to know the reasons why and the answers to and the
    people who and the places where and the days when,
    in memory of the bitter hours when we discovered we
    were black and poor and small and different and
    nobody cared and nobody wondered and nobody
    understood;

For the boys and girls who grew in spite of these things to be
    man and woman, to laugh and dance and sing and
    play and drink their wine and religion and success, to
    marry their playmates and bear children and then die
    of consumption and anemia and lynching;

For my people thronging 47th Street in Chicago and Lenox Avenue in New York and Rampart Street in New Orleans, lost disinherited dispossessed and happy people filling the cabarets and taverns and other people's pockets needing bread and shoes and milk and land and money and something—something all our own;

For my people walking blindly spreading joy, losing time being lazy, sleeping when hungry, shouting when burdened, drinking when hopeless, tied and shackled and tangled among ourselves by the unseen creatures who tower over us omnisciently and laugh;

For my people blundering and groping and floundering in the dark of churches and schools and clubs and societies, associations and councils and committees and conventions, distressed and disturbed and deceived and devoured by money-hungry glory-craving leeches, preyed on by facile force of state and fad and novelty, by false prophet and holy believer;

For my people standing staring trying to fashion a better way from confusion, from hypocrisy and misunderstanding, trying to fashion a world that will hold all the people, all the faces, all the adams and eves and their countless generations;

Let a new earth rise. Let another world be born. Let a bloody peace be written in the sky. Let a second generation full of courage issue forth; let a people loving freedom come to growth. Let a beauty full of healing and a strength of final clenching be the pulsing in our spirits and our blood. Let the martial songs be written, let the dirges disappear. Let a race of men now rise and take control.

Margaret Walker's "For My People" is not a poem that can be con-
sumed in a quick and dismissive reading. It invites multiple possible readings. A cultural-criticism orientation to reading the poem does not promote a privileged set of values. "For My People" converses with issues of
race, and these are complicated issues with political and historical and
ethical ramifications.

A teacher taking a reader-response approach to the poem might
ask students: What do you think this poem is about? What are your personal responses to the poem? What experiences with racism have you
had? A teacher taking a semiotics approach to the poem might address
the prosaic quality of the poem, and the repetitious beginning of each
stanza, and the aural and visual signifiers which constitute the shocking
experiences of racism. A teacher taking a deconstructive approach to the
poem might ask his or her students to focus on the intertextual connections between the poem and African-American traditions of gospel music and oratory and rap music. Each of these orientations is useful as a
way to open up the poetic text, but the cultural-criticism orientation
allows the teacher to connect the poem to the world. For example, the
poem can be compared to the speeches of Martin Luther King, Jr. and
Malcolm X, or to the films of Spike Lee, or the representation of African-
Americans on television and in advertising and in the popular culture.
Some students might investigate the history of African-Americans, including slavery and the long struggle for civil rights.

Teachers could also ask their students to consider the final stanza
with its contested meanings. The narrator issues a call for "a bloody peace."
The oxymoron rings with violence. The narrator's anger expressed in a
long catalogue of injustice and cruelty and loss is understood in the final
stanza as the motivation for a manifesto: "Let a beauty full/of healing
and strength of final clenching be the/pulsing in our spirits and our
blood." It is possible to read words like "beauty" and "healing" and feel a
strong sense of support for the narrator's ambitions, but the phrase
"strength of final clenching" jolts the reader into an awareness that the
narrator is calling for an end to the racial injustice that describes African-American history by inviting a violent wresting of power: "Let the/
martial songs be written, let the dirges disappear./Let a race of men now
rise and take control." Some readers who admire the peaceful efforts of

Martin Luther King, Jr. to create civil rights might be shocked by the tone of the poem. Other readers who admire the militant efforts of Malcolm X or the Black Panthers might respond differently to the narrator's voice. The poem will be read differently in different times by different readers. A cultural criticism orientation does not privilege or sanction a particular reading; instead the poem opens up spaces for conflicting and contested readings. What does it mean to be part of a race? How does membership in a race construct and constrain one's sense of identity? Is it possible to transform the identity that is inscribed by race? How can a person of one race know the experiences of a person of another race? How does racial identity lead to oppression? How can positive and negative constructions of race that lead to inequality be deconstructed and reconstructed in more equitable ways? With regard to issues of racial identity and violence, who is violated? Who is violent? Who is the violator, and what is violence? Margaret Walker's "For My People" does not shy away from these tough questions concerning racial identity and relationships. Walker compels readers to think again about how culture, history, politics, and commerce delineate and propagate and sustain the identities and roles of people by separating them into categories of race.

ACTIVITY

Many of the exercises suggested in previous sections could be modified to explore issues of race because issues of race include a wide range of social, historical, economic, cultural, and political issues informed by historicism, Marxism, feminism, and post-colonialism. But for the final exercises in the book, I recommend that students undertake an independent study project that examines issues of race from autobiographical perspectives. Students can research and write about their own experiences as people who have particular racial identities. All people have either been treated unjustly because of their racial identity, or they have responded to others in specific ways because of their racial identity. A potential danger in an autobiographical exercise is that a person might write the autobiography in order to sustain a position of power and dominance. It is impossible to escape entirely one's culturally inscribed racial identity, and when that identity provides a position of privilege and dominance, there might be a strong opposition to undermining that position with too much questioning. Nevertheless, if students are going to investigate how identity is racially defined, then they need to confront with courage and conviction and compassion experiences of racial identity, including their own. In her provocative poem "ITCOTU," Chrystos describes "this dangerous disease, whose anagram stands for I'm The Center Of The Universe." (Chrystos, 1995, 5) Characteristics of this disease include "inability to listen to others for longer than 3 minutes; the false concept that one's own ideas are superior to all others; the pitiful belief that control of others is paramount to one's own sanity." (5) Though it is not possible to throw off one's racial identity as if it were a costume, it is possible to deconstruct the subject positions of domination and privilege that are frequently taken for granted as part of one's racial identity. Since racial identity is constructed, it can be deconstructed and reconstructed. Poems like Margaret Walker's "For My People" or Jeannette Armstrong's "History Lesson" provide unsettling textual spaces for readers to confront tough questions concerning the construction of identity along racial lines. Instead of writing their own autobiographies, some students might choose to read the autobiographies of people of other races, or research the autobiographies of local people from different races. Out of these autobiographical explorations, students can then compose a personal creative project, such as a collection of poems, collage, video, audio-recording, tapestry, drama, or craft, which represents their autobiographical understanding of issues of race.

Afterword

I have written this book as a poet and a teacher, the one role informing and complementing the other. I hope that my explanations of the theoretical perspectives and strategies for teaching poetry will help readers enter the world of poetry, as well as enter the world through poetry. I hope that poets and teachers and students will revel together in the emotional and intellectual and social experience of poetry. The title *Teaching to Wonder* rings with grand promise, but I am confident that if teachers and students work together through the proposals in this book, they will know the power of poetry in their lives. My goal for this book is not to explain poetry, but to invite readers into the experience of poetry. By focusing our attention on our initial personal and subjective responses to poems, and then developing our literary competence as readers of poems by paying attention to the ways that poems work as texts, and then learning to deconstruct the multiple meanings of poetic texts, and finally connecting our personal responses to the larger contexts of the world in which poems communicate, we will know intimately the powerful pleasures of poetry. In these final few words I return to the question asked at the beginning of the book, What is a poem? I offer the following suggestions, and invite you to continue exploring the ways of looking at a poem.

Ninety-Nine Ways of Looking at a Poem

A poem is a song of silence.
A poem is a meadow of wildflowers.
A poem is the view from the patio on a summer morning.

A poem is the union of noun, conjunction, preposition, adjective, adverb, pronoun, verb.

A poem is writing light(ly).

A poem is a gift.

A poem is hope/full.

A poem is a love letter sent to another, to the world.

A poem is a construction of letters, grammar, words, syntax.

A poem is longing for the original difficulty.

A poem is geomancy, throwing lines of letters in the air, seeking shapes.

A poem is walking a tightrope over the falls.

A poem is visceral, awash with the body, one with the body.

A poem is a space for lingering.

A poem is babble and doodle.

A poem is geography, writing the earth.

A poem is a cacophonous chorus.

A poem is what can't be said.

A poem is the wasp that flies in and out of my patio.

A poem is storing and storying the past.

A poem is heart/full with the systolic and diastolic rhythm of the heart.

A poem is the unmapped space beyond the alphabet.

A poem is edible, bids savouring.

A poem is a hermeneut's heresy.

A poem is the song of sparrows in the autumn morning.

A poem is possibilities without end.

A poem is a rejuvenated cliché.

A poem is geometry, seeking connections among points, lines, and planes.

A poem is living un/grammatically.

A poem is prophecy.

A poem is knowing the wonder of the universe.

A poem is made with the hands and conjured with the spirit.

A poem is always politic, always political.

A poem is the lie of logic with thoughts and emotions scattered.

A poem is mystical music and musings.

A poem is an architect's dream.

A poem is truthful with wild laughter.

A poem is gramarye, fired in the spirit of necromancy and alchemy.

A poem is a fragrant fiction.
A poem is a guide for reading the stars.
A poem is falling in and out of and through love.
A poem is a reminder to become somebody else.
A poem is a life preserver thrown out to the world.
A poem is an urgent memo to look, smell, touch, listen, taste.
A poem is the subject and the predicate, changing places.
A poem is a space for knowing what is not known.
A poem is something, everything, anything.
A poem is a song for mourning in the evening and dancing in the morning.
A poem is refusing to answer the telephone just because it is ringing.
A poem is the scent of living poetically.
A poem is a visit to the grocery store to eat the free samples.
A poem is a textual affair.
A poem is a plea for pardon from the sentence.
A poem is a refusal to discuss the weather.
A poem is good news and bad news.
A poem is the dregs of coffee left in the basket after percolating.
A poem is juggling with words.
A poem is a long quest, a longer question.
A poem is humus, alive with the earth.
A poem is reading between the lines.
A poem is stirring the muddy bottom of a slough.
A poem is a warning of danger.
A poem is divining for truth with a forked stick.
A poem is a textual tease.
A poem is a story with holes, a reminder that the whole story is never told.
A poem is what remains to be said when everything has been said.
A poem is a fragment, an artifact.
A poem is truth with chaos in its heart.
A poem is a moonstruck creation spinning out infinitely.
A poem is a litter of letters.
A poem is finding new uses for conjunctions and prepositions.
A poem is a convention for contravening convention.

A poem is writing the unwritten sentence.
A poem is the word-woven world.
A poem is the spell conjured in every effort to spell a poem.
A poem is a network of highways and bridges and signs.
A poem is a keening kazoo.
A poem is a chain of words, a train of worlds.
A poem is a liminal space for dancing and laughing.
A poem is speaking in tongues, wandering in the alphabet.
A poem is the rumination of margins.
A poem is attention-seeking.
A poem is an echo.
A poem is intimate with the ligaments, muscles, and cartilages of the larynx.
A poem is living without punctuation.
A poem is a whisper of desire.
A poem is the voice of vision, and the vision of voice.
A poem is standing in a field of buttercups.
A poem is a tangle of lines.
A poem is a trumpet of thunder calling the calm.
A poem is a midnight candle on a window sill.
A poem is a packet of seeds.
A poem is an ample space for drawing close and hiding away.
A poem is a path of stones in a river.
A poem is the way of return.
A poem is alphabet soup, a brew for conjuring.
A poem is an ecotone, the place of tension where life abounds.
A poem is the trace of a sojourn in the wilderness.
A poem is words, even these words.

Recommended Anthologies

Adoff, Arnold, ed. 1968. *I Am the Darker Brother: An Anthology of Modern Poems by Black Americans.* New York: Collier Books.

Ahenakew, Freda, Brenda Gardipy, and Barbara Lafond, eds. 1993. *Native Voices.* Toronto: McGraw-Hill Ryerson.

Alford, Edna and Claire Harris, eds. 1992. *Kitchen Talk: Contemporary Women's Prose and Poetry.* Red Deer, Alberta: Red Deer College Press.

Allen, Robert, ed. 1987. *The Lyric Paragraph: A Collection of Canadian Prose Poems.* Montreal: DC Books.

Atwood, Margaret, ed. 1982. *The New Oxford Book of Canadian Verse in English.* Toronto: Oxford University Press.

Benedikt, Michael, ed. 1976. *The Prose Poem: An International Anthology.* New York: Dell.

Bierhorst, John, ed. 1983. *The Sacred Path: Spells, Prayers and Power Songs of the American Indians.* New York: William Morrow.

Birney, Earle et al. 1972. *Four Parts Sand: New Canadian Poets: Concrete Poems.* N.p.: Oberon Press.

Black, Ayama, ed. 1992. *Voices: Canadian Writers of African Descent.* Toronto: HarperCollins.

Bly, Robert, James Hillman, and Michael Meade, eds. 1992. *The Rag and Bone Shop of the Heart: Poems for Men.* New York: HarperCollins.

Bowering, George, ed. 1983. *The Contemporary Canadian Poem Anthology.* 4 vols. Toronto: Coach House Press.

Bowler, Berjouhi, ed. 1970. *The Word As Image.* London: Studio Vista.

Cameron, Bob, Margaret Hogan, and Patrick Lashmar, eds. 1983. *Poetry in Focus.* Toronto: Globe/Modern Curriculum Press.

Carson, Robert, ed. 1979. *The Waterfront Writers: The Literature of Work.* San Francisco: Harper and Row.

Chace, William M. and Peter Collier, eds. 1985. *An Introduction to Literature.* San Diego: Harcourt Brace Jovanovich.

Charlesworth, Roberta, ed. 1975. *Imagine Seeing You Here: A World of Poetry, Lively and Lyrical.* Toronto: Oxford University Press.

Cockburn, Robert and Robert Gibbs, eds. 1974. *Ninety Seasons: Modern Poems from the Maritimes.* Toronto: McClelland and Stewart.

Crozier, Lorna and Patrick Lane, eds. 1995. *Breathing Fire: Canada's New Poets.* Madeira Park, B.C.: Harbour Publishing.

Dalton, Mary et al., eds. 1995. *Wild on the Crest: Poems of the Sea, Newfoundland and Labrador.* St. John's, Newfoundland: Jeroboam Books.

Duffy, Carol Ann, ed. 1993. *I Wouldn't Thank You for a Valentine: Poems for Young Feminists.* New York: H. Holt.

Enright, D. J., ed. 1980. *The Oxford Book of Contemporary Verse 1945-1980.* Oxford: Oxford University Press.

Ferlinghetti, Lawrence, ed. 1995. *City Lights Pocket Poets Anthology.* San Francisco: City Lights Books.

Field, Edward, ed. 1979. *A Geography of Poets: An Anthology of the New Poetry.* Toronto: Bantam.

Footman, Jennifer, ed. 1995. *An Invisible Accordion: A Canadian Poetry Association Anthology.* Fredericton: Broken Jaw Press.

Geddes, Gary, ed. 1996. *Twentieth Century Poetry and Poetics.* 4th ed. Toronto: Oxford University Press.

Gensler, Kinereth and Nina Nyhart, eds. 1978. *The Poetry Connection.* New York: Teachers and Writers.

Giles, Mary E. and Kathryn Hohlwein, ed. 1981. *Enter the Heart of the Fire: A Collection of Mystical Poems.* Sacramento: California State University Press.

Gilbert, Sandra M. and Susan Gubar, eds. 1985. *The Norton Anthology of Literature by Women: The Tradition in English.* New York: W. W. Norton.

Gordon, Ruth, ed. 1995. *Pierced by a Ray of Sun: Poems about the Times We Feel Alone.* New York: HarperCollins.

Green, Rayna, ed. 1984. *That's What She Said: Contemporary Poetry and Fiction by Native American Women.* Bloomington: Indiana University Press.

Harrison, Michael and Christopher Stuart-Clark, ed. 1989. *Peace and War: A Collection of Poems.* Oxford: Oxford University Press.

Heaney, Seamus and Ted Hughes, eds. 1982. *The Rattle Bag: An Anthology of Poetry.* London: Faber and Faber.

Heyen, William, ed. 1984. *The Generation of 2000: Contemporary American Poets.* Princeton: Ontario Review Press.

Hirschfelder, Arlene B. and Beverly R. Singer, eds. 1992. *Rising Voices: Writings of Young Native Americans.* New York: Charles Scribner's Sons.

Hobson, Geary, ed. 1980. *The Remembered Earth: An Anthology of Contemporary Native American Literature.* Albuquerque: University of New Mexico Press.

Horsley, Mike, ed. *Reef, Palm and Star: Poetry from Nations of the Pacific.* Sydney, Australia: St. Clair Press, 1995.

Hunter, J. Paul, ed. 1996. *The Norton Introduction to Poetry.* 6th ed. New York: W. W. Norton, 1996.

Iveson, Margaret, John Oster, and Jill McClay, eds. 1990. *Literary Experiences.* Vol 2. Scarborough, ON: Prentice-Hall Canada.

Janeczko, Paul B., ed. 1991. *Preposterous Poems of Youth.* New York: Orchard Books.

————, ed. 1993. *Looking for Your Name: A Collection of Contemporary Poems.* New York: Orchard Books.

Junkins, Donald, ed. 1976. *The Contemporary World Poets.* New York: Harcourt Brace Jovanovich.

Kirkland, Glen and Richard Davies, eds. 1984. *Inside Poetry.* Don Mills: Academic Press Canada.

Klonsky, Milton, ed. 1975. *Speaking Pictures: A Gallery of Pictorial Poetry from the Sixteenth Century to the Present.* New York: Harmony Books.

Knudson, R.R. and May Swenson, eds. 1988. *American Sports Poems.* New York: Orchard Books.

Koch, Kenneth and Kate Farrell, ed. 1981. *Sleeping on the Wing: An Anthology of Modern Poetry with Essays on Reading and Writing.* New York: Random House.

LaDuke, Janice and Steve Luxton, eds. 1983. *Full Moon: An Anthology of Canadian Women Poets.* Dunvegan, Ontario: Quadrant Editions.

Lee, Dennis, ed. 1985. *The New Canadian Poets 1970-1985.* Toronto: McClelland and Stewart.

McCullough, Frances, ed. 1984. *Love Is Like the Lion's Tooth: An Anthology of Love Poems.* New York: Harper and Row.

McGann, Jerome J., ed. 1993. *The New Oxford Book of Romantic Verse.* Oxford: Oxford University Press.

McGifford, Diane and Judith Kearns, ed. *Shakti's Words: An Anthology of South Asian Canadian Women's Poetry.* 2nd ed. Toronto: TSAR, 1993.

McNeil, Florence, ed. 1983. *Here Is a Poem: An Anthology of Canadian Poetry.* N.p.:The League of Canadian Poets.

Myers, Jack and Roger Weingarten, eds. 1984. *New America Poets of the 80's.* Green Harbor, MA: Wampeter Press.

Nemiroff, Greta Hofmann, ed. 1993. *Gender Issues.* Toronto: McGraw-Hill Ryerson.

Nims, John Frederick, ed. 1990. *Sappho to Valery: Poems in Translation.* Fayetteville: University of Arkansas Press.

Norris, Ken and Bob Hilderley, eds. 1988. *Poets 88: 30 New Canadian Poets Under 30.* Kingston: Quarry Press.

Nye, Naomi Shihab, ed. 1992. *This Same Sky: A Collection of Poems from around the World.* New York: Four Winds Press.

Okpewho, Isidore, ed. 1985. *The Heritage of African Poetry.* New York: Longman.

Oster, John, Margaret Iveson, and Jill McClay, eds. 1989. *Literary Experiences.* Vol. 1. Scarborough, ON: Prentice-Hall Canada.

Page, P.K., ed. 1980. *To Say the Least: Canadian Poets from A to Z.* Toronto: University of Toronto Press.

Peck, Richard, ed. 1976. *Pictures That Storm Inside My Head.* New York: Avon.

Plotz, Helen, ed. 1982. *Saturday's Children: Poems of Work*. New York: Greenwillow Books.

Rexroth, Kenneth, ed. 1971. *One Hundred Poems from the Chinese*. New York: New Directions.

Rosengarten, Herbert and Amanda Goldrick-Jones, eds. 1993. *The Broadview Anthology of Poetry*. Peterborough: Broadview Press.

Ruger, Hendrika, ed. 1989. *Dutch Voices: A Collection of Stories and Poems by Dutch Canadians*. Windsor, ON: Netherlandic Press.

Rumens, Carol, ed. 1985. *Making for the Open: The Chatto Book of Post-Feminist Poetry 1964-1984*. London: Chatto and Windus.

Saliani, Dom, ed. 1991. *Poetry Alive: Perspectives*. Toronto: Copp Clark Pitman.

Saunders, Walter, David Segatlhe, and B. L. Leshoai, eds. 1990. *Blue Black: And Other Poems*. Southern Africa: Hodder and Stoughton Educational.

Shapcott, Thomas, ed. 1976. *Contemporary American and Australian Poetry*. St. Lucia, Queensland: University of Queensland Press.

Smith, Charles, ed. 1985. *Sad Dances in a Field of White*. Toronto: Is Five Press.

Solt, Mary Ellen, ed. 1970. *Concrete Poetry: A World View*. Bloomington: Indiana University Press, 1970.

Stallworthy, Jon, ed. 1984. *The Oxford Book of War Poetry*. Oxford: Oxford University Press.

Vendler, Helen, ed. 1985. *The Harvard Book of Contemporary American Poetry*. Cambridge: Harvard University Press.

Wagner-Martin, Linda and Cathy N. Davidson, eds. 1995. *The Oxford Book of Women's Writing in the United States*. Oxford: Oxford University Press.

Wayman, Tom, ed. 1991. *Paperwork: Contemporary Poems from the Job*. Madeira Park, BC: Harbour Publishing.

Wharton, Calvin and Tom Wayman, eds. 1989. *East of Main: An Anthology of Poems from East Vancouver*. Vancouver: Pulp Press.

Williams, John, ed. 1990. *English Renaissance Poetry: A Collection of Shorter Poems from Skelton to Jonson*. 2nd ed. Fayetteville: University of Arkansas Press.

Wilner, Isabel, ed. 1977. *The Poetry Troupe: An Anthology of Poems to Read Aloud*. New York: Charles Scribner's Sons.

Worsnop, Chris, ed. 1994. *Popular Culture*. Toronto: McGraw-Hill Ryerson.

Wowk, Jerry and Ted Jason, eds. 1993. *Multiculturalism*. Toronto: McGraw-Hill Ryerson.

References

Ashcroft, Bill, Gareth Griffiths, and Helen Tiffin. 1989. *The Empire Writes Back: Theory and Practice in Post-Colonial Literatures*. London: Routledge.

Attridge, Derek. 1982. *The Rhythms of English Poetry*. London: Longman.

Barrow, Robin. 1984. *Giving Teaching Back to Teachers: A Critical Introduction to Curriculum Theory*. London: Althouse Press.

Belsey, Catherine. 1980. *Critical Practice*. London: Methuen.

Benedikt, Michael. 1976. *The Prose Poem: An International Anthology*. New York: Dell.

Bleich, David. 1980. Epistemological Assumptions in the Study of Response. *Reader-Response Criticism*, edited by Jane P. Tompkins. Baltimore: Johns Hopkins.

Bogdan, Deanne. 1984. Pygmalion as Pedagogue: Subjectivist Bias in the Teaching of Literature. *English Education* 16: 67-75.

Bonhoffer, Dietrich. 1967. *Letters and Papers from Prison*. Edited by Eberhard Bethge. New York: Macmillan.

Bowering, George. 1983. The End of the Line. *The Contemporary Canadian Poem Anthology*. Vol. 4. Toronto: Coach House Press: 347-353.

Bremner, Charles C. 1984. *The Working Tools of English Prosody*. Victoria: N. p.

Brenkman, John. 1985. The Concrete Utopia of Poetry: Blake's "A Poison Tree." *Lyric Poetry: Beyond New Criticism*, edited by Chaviva Hosek and Patricia Parker. Ithaca: Cornell.

Chrystos. 1995. *Fire Power*. Vancouver: Press Gang Publishers.

Coles, Nicholas. 1986. Democraticizing Literature: Issues in Teaching Working-Class Literature. *College English* 48: 664-680.

Danesi, Marcel. 1994. *Messages and Meanings: An Introduction to Semiotics*. Toronto: Canadian Scholars' Press.

De Man, Paul. 1985. Lyrical Voice in Contemporary Theory: Riffaterre and Jauss. *Lyric Poetry: Beyond New Criticism*, edited by Chaviva Hosek and Patricia Parker. Ithaca: Cornell.

Dias, Patrick. 1985. Understanding Response to Poetry: Attending to the Process. *Highway One* 8.1, 2: 209-219.

———. 1986. Making Sense of Poetry: Patterns of Response Among Canadian and British Secondary School Pupils. *English in Education* 20.2: 44-52.

Eagleton, Terry. 1976. *Marxism and Literary Criticism*. London: Methuen.
————. 1983. *Literary Theory: An Introduction*. Oxford: Basil Blackwell.
Easthope, Antony. 1983. *Poetry as Discourse*. London: Methuen.
Eliot, T. S. 1971. *Four Quartets*. San Diego: Harcourt Brace Jovanovich.
Enright, D. J., ed. 1980. *The Oxford Book of Contemporary Verse 1945-1980*. Oxford.
Fish, Stanley. 1980. *Is There a Text in This Class?* Cambridge, Mass.: Harvard.
Francis, Robert. 1977. *Fifty Contemporary Poets: The Creative Process*, edited by Alberta J. Turner. New York: David McKay.
Galloway, Priscilla. 1980. *What's Wrong with High School English? . . . It's Sexist, Un-Canadian, Outdated*. Toronto: OISE Press.
Giroux, Henry A. 1981. Toward a New Sociology of Curriculum. *Curriculum and Instruction*, edited by Henry A. Giroux, Anthony N. Penn, and William F. Pinar. Berkeley: McCutchan.
————. 1984. Rethinking the Language of Schooling, *Language Arts* 61.1: 34-39.
Gregory, Gerald. 1984. Community-Published Working-Class Writing in Context. *Changing English: Essays for Harold Rosen*, edited by Margaret Meek and Jane Miller. London: Heinemann Educational Books.
Grierson, Phil and Chris Richardson. 1982. Introducing Language Studies. *English in Education* 16.2: 12-16.
Gutteridge, Don. 1983. The Coherence of Consonance in Poetry in English. *English Quarterly* 16.3: 3-10.
Hansen, Tom. 1980. Letting Language Do: Some Speculations on Finding Found Poems. *College English* 42: 271-282.
Hayhoe, Mike. 1984. Sharing the Headstart: An Exploratory Approach to Teaching Poetry. *English Quarterly* 17.3: 39-44.
Hurry, David. 1986. Necessary Rhymes (with Saussure). *English in Education* 20.3: 60-68.
Levine, Josie. You Liar, Miss. *Changing English: Essays for Harold Rosen*, edited by Margaret Meek and Jane Miller. London: Heinemann Educational Books, 1984.
Macherey, Pierre. 1977. Problems of Reflection. *Literature, Society and the Sociology of Literature*, edited by Francis Barker et al. Colchester: University of Essex.
Norris, Christopher. 1982. *Deconstruction: Theory and Practice*. London: Methuen.
O'Neill, Marnie. 1993. Teaching Literature as Cultural Criticism. *English Quarterly* 25.1: 19-25.
Orr, Leonard. 1986. Intertextuality and the Cultural Text in Recent Semiotics. *College English* 48: 811-823.
Probst, Robert E. 1984. *Adolescent Literature: Response and Analysis*. Columbus: C. E. Merrill.
Quirk, Randolph. 1982. Foreword to *The Rhythms of English Poetry* by Derek Attridge. London: Longman.
Rosenblatt, Louise. 1978. *The Reader, the Text, the Poem*. Carbondale: Southern Illinois UP.

Schmidt, Tom. 1981. The Poetry Experience. *The Poetry Reading: A Contemporary Compendium on Language and Performance,* edited by Stephen Vincent and Ellen Zweig. San Francisco: Momo's Press.

Scholes, Robert. 1982. *Semiotics and Interpretation.* New Haven: Yale.

Searchlights. 1970. Vol. 1. Agincourt: Book Society of Canada.

Showalter, Elaine, ed. 1986. *The New Feminist Criticism: Essays on Women, Literature, and Theory.* London: Virago.

Solt, Mary Ellen, ed. 1970. *Concrete Poetry: A World View.* Bloomington: Indiana.

Strenski, Ellen and Nancy Giller Esposito. 1980. The Poet, the Computer, and the Classroom. *College English* 42: 142-150.

Wallace, Ronald. 1981. Babble and Doodle: Introducing Students to Poetry. *College English* 43: 556-568.

Webb, Edwin. 1985. The Sounds of Poetry. *Use of English* 37.1: 57-67.

Willinsky, John. 1990. *The New Literacy: Redefining Reading and Writing in the Schools.* New York: Routledge.

Acknowledgements

Every effort has been made to acknowledge all sources of the poems reprinted in this book. The publishers would be grateful if any errors or omissions were pointed out, so they may be corrected in future printings. Acknowledgement is gratefully made for the use of the following poems. "The Courage to Love," unpublished poem by Carl Leggo. "The Mystic East" from *Syntax* by Robin Blaser, published by Talon Books (1983). "Everything you ever wanted to know about philosophy, but was too embarrassed to ask," unpublished poem by Carl Leggo. "Moment in Autumn," from *Prisoner of the Rain: Poems in Prose* by Michael Bullock, published by Third Eye Publications (1983). Permission granted by the author. "The Elm Log" from *Stories and Prose Poems by Alexander Solzhenitsyn*, translated by Michael Glenny. Translation copyright © 1970, 1971 by Michael Glenny. Reprinted by permission of Farrar, Straus & Giroux , and Claude Durand. "The Computer's First Birthday Card" from *Collected Poems* by Edwin Morgan, published by Carcanet Press Ltd. "Point of View," unpublished poem by Carl Leggo. "Mountain Boogie" from *Mountain Tea* by Peter van Toorn. Used by permission of the publishers, McClelland & Stewart, Toronto. "Ping pong," by Eugen Gomringer, from *Concrete Poetry: A World View,* ed. Mary Ellen Solt, published by Indian University Press (1968). "Put put," unpublished poem by Carl Leggo. "Silent Poem" reprinted from *Robert Francis: Collected Poems, 1936-1976* (Amherst: University of Massachusetts Press, 1976), copyright © 1976 by Robert Francis. "I Still Hear the Bell Ringing" from *Growing Up Perpendicular on the Side of a Hill* by Carl Leggo, published by Killick Press (1994). "th wundrfulness uv th mountees our secret police" from *Sailor* by bill bissett, published by Talon Books (1978). "Mother," from *Selected Poems* by Andrew Waterman, published by Carcanet Press (1986). "Running on Empty," © 1981 Robert Phillips by arrangement with Wieser & Wieser, Inc. from *Running on Empty: New Poems* by Robert Phillips. "San Francisco" from *The Pill Versus the Springhill Mine Disaster,* © 1968 by Richard Brautigan. Renewal © 1996 Ianthe Brautigan Swensen. "The Addict" from *Live or Die* by Anne Sexton. Copyright © 1966 by Anne Sexton. Reprinted by permission of Houghton Mifflin Co. All rights reserved. "Dietrich Bonhoffer at the Gallows" from *Collected Poems of Raymond Souster,* vol. 4, by Raymond Souster, published by Oberon Press (1983). "The Fist" from *Sea Grapes* by Derek Walcott, published by Jonathan Cape (1976). "Epilogue" by Denise Levertov, from *Life in the Forest.* Copyright © 1978 by Denise Levertov. Reprinted by permission of New Directions Publishing Corp. "Track" by Tomas Tranströmer Reprinted from *Friends, You Drank Some Darkness: Three Swedish Poets,* trans. Robert Bly, published by Beacon Press (1975). Copyright 1975 by Robert Bly. Reprinted with his permission. "To Julia de Burgos" by Julia de Burgos, translated by Grace Schulman, first published in *The Nation* (1972). "This is a Photograph of Me" from *The Circle Game* by Margaret Atwood, published by The House of Anansi Press. Reprinted with the permission of Stoddart Publishing Co. Limited . "A Wonder," by Sakutaro Hagiwara, from *The Prose Poem: An International Anthology,* ed. Michael Benedikt, published by Dell (1976). "The Hanging Man" from *Ariel* by Sylvia Plath, reprinted by permission of harperCollins Publishers, Inc. Copyright © 1965 by Ted Hughes. "Eve" from *Collected Poems: The Two Seasons* by Dorothy Livesay, published by McGraw-Hill Ryerson. "Pose" from *Burning Stone* by Zoë Landale, published by Ronsdale Press (1995). "Birdsong" from *I Never Saw Another Butterfly* (anon.), Volavkova, H. ed., published by McGraw-Hill (1964). "Growing Up Perpendicular on the Side of a Hill" from *Growing Up Perpendicular on the Side of a Hill* by Carl Leggo, published by Killick (1994). "Checking the Doors," unpublished poem by Renee Norman. "History Lesson" from *Breathtracks* by Jeannette Armstrong, published by Theytus Books. "For My People" from *For My People* by Margaret Walker, published by Yale University Press (1942). Reprinted by permission of the author.

Index